NETARY NOISE

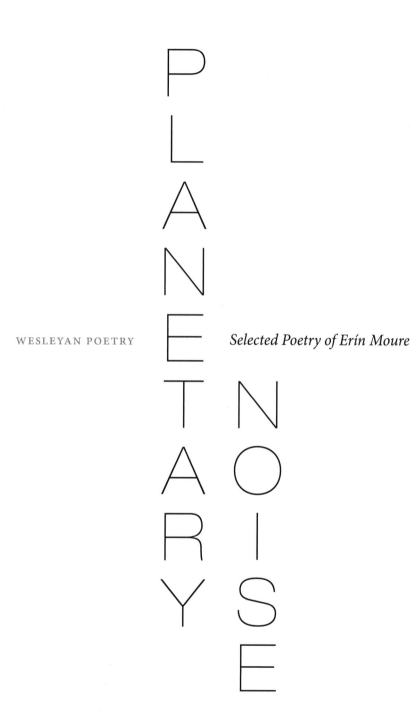

PLANETARY NOISE

WESLEYAN POETRY

Selected Poetry of Erín Moure

EDITED BY SHANNON MAGUIRE   Wesleyan University Press   Middletown, Connecticut

Wesleyan University Press

Middletown CT 06459

www.wesleyan.edu/wespress

© 2017 Erín Moure

Introduction © 2017 Shannon Maguire

Manufactured in the United States of America

Designed by Mindy Basinger Hill

Typeset in Minion Pro

Library of Congress Cataloging-in-Publication Data

Names: Moure, Erín, 1955– author. | Maguire, Shannon, editor.

Title: Planetary noise / selected poetry of Erín Moure ;
    edited by Shannon Maguire.

Description: Middletown, Connecticut : Wesleyan University Press, [2017] |
Series: Wesleyan poetry

Identifiers: LCCN 2016038491 (print) | LCCN 2016044220 (ebook) | ISBN
    9780819576941 (cloth : alk. paper) | ISBN 9780819576958 (pbk. : alk. paper) |
    ISBN 9780819576965 (ebook)

Classification: LCC PR9199.3.M67 A6 2017 (print) | LCC PR9199.3.M67 (ebook) |
DDC 811/.54—dc23

LC record available at https://lccn.loc.gov/2016038491

5   4   3   2   1

This project is supported in part by an award from
the National Endowment for the Arts.

Contents

Erín Moure: Poetry as Planetary Noise

This is intertextuality where we are a very small part of
the intertext in the planetary and inter-planetary ecology . . .
Relativity, probability, chance—we are their subjects
and they are ours. PHYLLIS WEBB[1]

Erín Moure is one of English North America's most prolific and daring contemporary poets. Her work in and among languages has altered the conditions of possibility for poets of several generations—myself included. With her ear tilted close to the noise floor, Moure listens for patterns arising from contemporary Englishes and from "minor" languages such as Galician, and shifts language structures away from commerce so as to hear other possibilities, other tensions. In so doing, subjectivity, justice, and politics can be considered anew. Moure's work is transnational in scope; her lines transit from one articulated locality to arrive at or include another. Her poems attend, in various registers, to bodily capacities and fragilities as much as to the operations of power. Moure's poetry travels joyously through noise, and sometimes even *as* noise, via various channels and contexts, refusing absorption. For Moure, "Poetry is a limit case of language; it's language brought to its limits (which are usually in our own heads) where its workings are strained and its sinews are visible, and where its relationship with bodies and time and space can crack open" (*Montreal Review of Books*). Facing a Moure poem as a reader, I appreciate the disquieting rhythms, sudden symmetries, outlandish puns, and general pleasure caused by roiling syntax and audacious neologisms. Even without knowing the majority of the languages that Moure draws on, I am compelled by the sounds and echoes that her poems amplify, and the patterns of letters and words that they make visible on the page.

Moure's work is critically acclaimed, and her fourth book, *Furious* (1988), won the Governor General's Award for Poetry—Canada's most prestigious national poetry award at that time, an equivalent of an American Pulitzer Prize. As of 2016, Moure's oeuvre includes seventeen collections of poetry (one collaborative), several chapbooks, a collection of essays, *My Beloved Wager: Essays from a Writing Practice* (2009), and a biopoetics, *Insecession,*

---

1. Phyllis Webb, "The Crannies of Matter: Texture in Robin Blaser's Later 'Image-Nations'" in *Nothing but Brush Strokes: Selected Prose of Phyllis Webb*, ed. Smaro Kamboureli (Edmonton: NeWest Press, 1995), 71.

that sonically relocates Chus Pato's *Secession*. In addition, Moure has translated works of poetry, theatre, literary criticism, and creative non-fiction from four languages—French, Galician, Spanish, and Portuguese—into English. As with her own work, her translations and essays are trailblazing and often push the boundaries of form and test the ideological limits of these discursive practices. Her other accolades include the Pat Lowther Memorial Award for *Domestic Fuel* (1985), and the A.M. Klein Award for Poetry for *WSW (West South West)* (1989) and for *Little Theatres* (2005). Her poetry has been translated into several languages, and two of her books are translated in full, *Little Theatres* into Galician and French, and *O Cadoiro* into German.

Moure most often engineers book-length networks of poems. Since *Search Procedures* (1996), which initiated her first trilogy, her work has been organized into groupings of books that probe a series of inquiries from different angles. Moure's interest in seriality is evinced as early as "Riel: In the Season of his Birth" from her first collection, *Empire York Street* (1979). Her early work shows her familiarity with Charles Olson's 1950 essay "Projective Verse," and as Heather Fitzgerald points out, "asthma is a defining . . . feature of her writing practice" (Fitzgerald, "Finesse into Mess" 115). The lung is one site that figures textural difference in Moure's oeuvre, and the ear is another site where differential textures—of several languages, of environmental "noise," and of heterogeneous voices—meet and mix. But the hands: "those organs of power and insistence, organs of tactility, *le toucher* . . . [o]rgans that write" (Moure, *My Beloved Wager* 92) are just as important and integrated into a poetics that refuses to erase difference, no matter the scale. For Moure, "the hand is also a sex organ" (*My Beloved Wager* 92) and the mouth is an organ of desire, of translation: a chamber of libidinous exchange between lungs and ears. Moure's poetic inquiries into bodily capacities and connections internalize as well as extend the field of composition. In Moure's work, the lines and trajectories in *language* emerge from a *body* in contact with its environment and cultural location(s). Moure herself points out:

> It is critical to consider the body not as self-enclosed and complete but as a coding practice; to understand, as Donna Haraway does, that what constitutes an organism or a machine is in fact indeterminate. They are coded by culture, oh yes, but there are ways to have agency and code back . . . I call the reader's attention in my work to missing words, repetitions, misspellings, and jarring representations—or not representations but designations: machine struggles and coalescences that construct selves

that collide, molecularize, pine, adopt, enjoy and confront a wide range of emotions and desires. I have no easy answers; I don't even look for ease. (*My Beloved Wager* 94–95)

Out of the disturbance of breath, of voice, Moure re(con)figures what counts as noise and what counts as signal. And she does this over and over again, calling fixed locations and sedimented identities and relations constantly into question, "coding back."

Digital literary innovator Michael Joyce was the first to read Moure's poetry as theoretically relevant to hypertextuality. In *Of Two Minds: Hypertext Pedagogy and Poetics* (1996), Joyce uses passages from poems in Moure's *Furious* and *WSW (West South West)* to clarify what hypertextuality is (180–181, 207). In other words, he treats her poetry as theoretical text—a very fruitful approach to Moure's oeuvre, and one that begs to be taken up more often (and not just on the subject of hypertextuality). For Joyce, a hypertext means "reading and writing in an order you choose, where the choices you make change the nature of what you read or write" (*Othermindedness* 38). This is an ethos embraced by Moure from *Furious* (1988) onward. Moure's use of noise—the part of communication that is deemed unwanted and unwelcome and yet is unavoidable—as both medium and ethical threshold in her poetry is very much related to the sorts of choices that frame Joyce's description of hypertext. Moure is a philosopher of cognition and the politics of reading, and her poetic works are the mode of her interdisciplinary inquiries. For the critics who have dismissed her work as "difficult" and "unintelligible"—and there have been several of those over the years, both in the popular press and in academic circles—critic and poet Jamie Dopp has useful advice:

> In reading Moure, then, it is important to be as receptive as possible
> to discomfort, to instability, to "the edge of confusion" that the poems
> invite the reader to inhabit. It is not always easy to be receptive. There is a
> tremendous disruptive energy in Moure's later work; it has the in-your-face
> celebratory quality of Hélène Cixous's Medusa laughing. (Dopp 269)

The "edge of confusion" is a threshold of particular importance in Moure's poetry. Many readers recognize and celebrate that as a thinker and worker in language, Moure is tireless, and her practice deeply engages with reading and listening as ethical modes of encounter. Moure's theories of citizenship and subjectivity have met with intense critical attention (Carrière, Dowling,

Fitzpatrick, MacDonald, Moyes, Rudy, Skibsrud), and recent articles have also drawn connections between Moure's poetics and queer affect theory (Moore, Williams and Marinkova).

Moure often responds to the work of other poets and philosophers as well as visual and theatre artists within her own texts, and it is not unusual to find suggestions for reading at the end of her own books. Some of her companions in letters include contemporary American poets C.D. Wright, Susan Howe, Myung Mi Kim, Lyn Hejinian, Rae Armantrout, Barbara Guest, Norma Cole; philosophers as diverse as Baruch Spinoza, Gilles Deleuze, Jacques Derrida, Emmanuel Levinas, Luce Irigaray, and Judith Butler; as well as edgy modernists such as Gertrude Stein, Fernando Pessoa, Federico García Lorca, Paul Celan, Samuel Beckett, Ingeborg Bachmann, Miklós Radnóti, Daniil Kharms, Heinrich Müller, and Jean-Luc Lagarce. Galician poet Chus Pato has been one of Moure's most important interlocutors in the twenty-first century.

Moure was born in Calgary, Alberta, Canada in 1955. At the age of twenty-four, she published her first full-length book, *Empire York Street* (1979), which was a finalist for the Governor General's Award for Poetry. Earlier, she attended the University of British Columbia in Vancouver as a Philosophy student, where the consequences of inhabiting a woman's body as one from which to write became painfully clear during her second year, in 1975. As she explains:

> I spent [time] in the mid-seventies living in a small room on York Avenue, attending UBC, supporting myself by working as a cook. "hazard of the occupation" was workshopped in Pat Lowther's class, which I attended until her murder, at which point I quit school and turned to cooking. What isolation and unease I felt in those days before . . . I started to explore my relationship to language itself! (Svendsen 263)

Pat Lowther was a working-class poet just gaining national acclaim in Canada, a rare achievement for a woman then. Moure enrolled in Pat Lowther's senior Creative Writing workshop (as a non-major) to have a woman mentor. But Lowther went missing a few weeks into the course, and was later found dead, murdered by her husband. This event reverberates subtly through Moure's oeuvre; in establishing her own practice, she had to confront "how a woman wanting to write can be a *territorial* impossibility" (*O Cidadán* 79). The university soon replaced Lowther with a male instructor, who in his first class wrote poetry on the blackboard in Latin, a language that Moure, raised Catholic, had felt barred from learning in school because of her gender. All of this, to Moure, augmented the gender violence of the situation.

After leaving university, Moure worked as a cook for CN Rail (later VIA Rail, the Canadian passenger train service) on trains between Vancouver and Winnipeg. Two decades later, she left VIA as Senior Officer of Customer Relations and Employee Communications, based in Montreal. She then worked as a freelance translator, editor, and communications specialist. Both her lower middle class roots and her expertise in communications are of great and ongoing importance to her poetics. In communications theory, noise is an interference in a communications channel, or involves those signals that are peripheral to the communication goal. Moure's poetic intervention takes noise as an object of attention, even desire: noise acts as a threshold of relationality. In *O Cidadán*, Moure clearly articulates this question as central to her poetic inquiry: "What if we listen to the noise and not the signal?" (102). From another poem in that collection, I draw the title for this volume:

When "my language" fails, only then can we detect signals that harken
to a porosity of borders or lability of zones . . . (across the entire
electromagnetic spectrum, not just the visual. as in *planetary noise*) . . .
(*O Cidadán* 79)

Moure adds that "*reading* (bodies or others) is itself always a kind of weak signal communication, a process of tapping signals that scarcely rise off the natural noise floor" (79). Poetry may be hard to hear in the din of globalized commerce, but in directing our attention towards what is deemed "planetary noise," to the "little theatres," Moure suggests we are better able to assume our civic responsibility.

Planetary Noise: Selected Poetry of Erín Moure is organized chronologically in seven sections that trace her poetic trajectories and shifting use of noise as a poetic medium and a tool of perception. The editing process has been collaborative: I proposed the theme and title and then we negotiated the contents, and our conversations affected decisions about inclusions. Moure curated "Polyresonances (Transborder Noise)" herself and contributed a postface on translation. Although this volume is organized with readers of poetry in mind, it will open productive ways of viewing Moure's oeuvre for readers from any field, expert and novice alike.

While living in Vancouver, Canada, from 1975 to 1985, Moure published *Empire, York Street* (1979), *Wanted Alive* (1983), and *Domestic Fuel* (1985), as well as a chapbook, *The Whisky Vigil* (1981), which included her line drawings. In search of a community of writers, Moure joined the Vancouver Industrial Writers' Union and did her early reading and writing in the restaurants and bars of Mount Pleasant and the Downtown Eastside—"Canada's poorest postal code"—alongside Tom Wayman, Phil Hall, Zoë Landale, Kate Braid, Calvin Wharton, and other members.

> Erín Moure: [I] read with those writers and we talked about that interface between poetry and the street a lot; I was always in favor of a more radical approach to poetry. Wayman's claim was that working people needed to see themselves in poetry, though I found my own railway coworkers were interested in far more than that. Also, the emphasis on working class in that writing excluded gay or lesbian consciousness, which was something that I at some point around 1980 could no longer deny as part of my work.

Moure published her second full-length collection in 1983; the following year, she left for Montreal and began a new phase of her writing that would soon include transnational collaborations, polylingual explorations, and a commitment to queer feminist analysis within her poetry.

The feminist literary awakening in North America was made possible by the groundwork done in women's collectives that, starting in the 1960s and '70s, founded and ran women's presses, bookstores, magazines and newsletters, as well as health clinics, women's shelters, campaigns for women's control over their own bodies, and anti-rape initiatives. This supporting network enabled inventiveness in the literary arena as well. Moure attended the *Women and Words, Les femmes et les mots* conference, held in Vancouver in 1983, one of the first feminist literary conferences in Canada. It was "a watershed event, [as] it represented the culmination of more than a decade of feminist activism on many fronts. It also inspired many more ongoing activities" (Butling and Rudy 2005, 24). For Moure, the event was as crucial for supplying key reading material as it was for sparking discussions with other women writers—Nicole Brossard, Claire Harris, France Théoret, Gail Scott, and many others—whose work demonstrated the poetic felicity of non-mimetic language.

Shortly after arriving in the city, Moure met translator Lucille Nelson at the Montreal branch of *Les femmes et les mots,* and they formed a two-person reading group to discuss Jacques Derrida's *Of Grammatology.* Gradually, Moure began to devour philosophy and gender theory on her own: along with the philosophers mentioned earlier, works by Gayatri Spivak, Jean-François Lyotard, Rosi Braidotti, Hélène Cixous, Julia Kristeva, and Elizabeth Grosz were prominent in her reading at that time. Notably as well, Cixous brought the fiction of Clarice Lispector to Moure's attention, which caused Moure to puzzle about its translation before she could read Portuguese.

This period of extensive reading led to the shift in Moure's own writing that began to surface in her Governor General's Award winning collection *Furious* (1988). The book opens with an epigraph from Kathy Acker's *Great Expectations*—a postmodern novel about gender, class, and narration—and ends with a section called "The Acts," in which Moure deconstructs the gender privilege operating in language structures, and its effect on poetry. Lesbian sexuality is figured as noise that disturbs even the structure of the line and the page: as "the howl" of grief and desire in "Rose" (37); as "the wings of the cicadas" (45); and as "the characteristic whelp or yelp / that says I've found something" in "Three Signs" (53). Twenty-six years later in *Insecession*, Moure suggests: "Poems activate more areas of the human cortex than do non-ambiguous speech, they bring excedent light and hormonal energy into the dark matter of the frontal cortex; when we read literature we equip our brains to deal with 'ambiguous speech'" (150). Noise and eroticism are irrevocably joined in Moure's poetry.

The poems selected for this section expose the major trajectories of Moure's poetics from thermodynamics to cross-species interactions to the relationship between death, writing, allergy, and translation, to the anarchic eruption of humor. These poems echo and refract in later books; Moure treats her writing over the years as material "subject to abrasion, deformation, collapse and passages" (*My Beloved Wager* 95) and thus as material ripe for reconfiguration and regeneration. From the very first poem of *Empire York Street* (1979), "february: turn toward spring" (10), environment is put before system when "the clutter / of words" is described as a "black noise / that typewriter makes // outside," situated between the writer and the birds. Insects—who appear dead between double frames but are about to wake up after winter hibernation—adjoin the writing body in the struggle and confusion of spring:

between double panes, dead
insects. wasp, wire-legged
spider, beetle, luminous flies
all on their shoulders in dusty
sill

when the true thaw begins,
& the equinox they will awake,
struggle for air.
flip again onto damaged legs to devour
dirt from the ledge, patch crackt
glass w/ mucous & wait (10)

The image of these damaged but productive insects echoes in "Snow Door" from *Furious* (1988):

Dead flies between the panes, winter flies that come to life when they warm
up, but go stupid from the freezing, & can't remember flight exactly, not exact
enough, they topple on their backs & spin & buzz. Having forgotten everything
except that they used to fly (19)

More obliquely, in "The Jewel" from *WSW*, sleep, frost, and darkness seem to promise a new form of perception or consciousness for the writing body:

The thyme in the mouth risen gorging the head full of sleep, I
wake up, am waking, my body alone naked house silent
around the wall, bed, drug of sleep, oh my drug
my hands warm tongue soft sheet in the mouth taste of thyme & silver
frost, on the window, light enters, the jewel light enters &
the darkness, begins (18)

The material of these poems echoes and resonates, and is reshaped, reframed and recalled in each phase of Moure's oeuvre. In her early work, noise represents the productive blindspot that leads to transformation and changes in perception. Noise is figured as the mechanical sound of the typewriter, as the "terrific noise of light   wakening" ("Bird," *Wanted Alive* 1983, 15), and as "the noise of the book" ("Philosophy of Language," *Domestic Fuel* 1985, 54). Listening for the echoes, a reader is asked to continually relocate her perceptions in relation to the movements of the poems. This relocation is a source of readerly pleasure.

With the success of *Furious,* Moure entered a fifteen-year period of intense output and stunning breakthroughs. Between the years 1989 and 2002, Moure published six collections as well as her acclaimed altered translation of Pessoa, *Sheep's Vigil by a Fervent Person,* and a co-translation (with Robert Majzels) of Nicole Brossard's *Installations.* Over the same period, queer activist networks were remapped in response to the HIV/AIDS epidemic, queer theory gained traction in the academy and the Canadian "censorship wars" saw the seizure of gay and lesbian reading materials by Canadian authorities at the US/Canada border. If Moure responded to these conditions by devising poetic methods to risk the limit of understanding, it was because conventional geopolitical and psychosocial mappings of the spaces where she lived were quite literally deadly.

WSW (West South West) (1989) and *Sheepish Beauty, Civilian Love* (1992) followed *Furious.* These books link poetic structures and processes to bodily ones. In her 1996 essay, "Speaking the Unspeakable: Responding to Censorship," Moure explains:

> The view of the body most akin to mine is Spinoza's, which I first encountered via Gilles Deleuze. Spinoza defines a body in two ways, which work in simultaneity: first as composed of particles, an infinite number of particles in motion or at rest, thus defined not by forms but by velocities; second, as a capacity for affecting or being affected by other bodies, so that part of a body's it-ness is its relationality. To me, there's a clear marker here for *community*—broadly speaking, all other beings we are in contact with— as an indispensable part of our definition of who we are as individuals. (*My Beloved Wager* 97)

These preoccupations with the relationship between individual and community informed her work in a trilogy of books: *Search Procedures* (1996), *A Frame of The Book / The Frame of A Book* (1999), and *O Cidadán* (2002). As Moure examines the many practices that create our world, from our most intimate interfaces at our cellular and neurological limits to our cultural and political exchanges, she introduces languages other than English—French,

Galician, Portuguese, Spanish—into the poems. Lexicons derived from science and technology likewise alter the tension in Moure's texts of this period, and she draws upon noise's productive capacity in order to create new words. *O Cidadán*, the final and most complex book in the trilogy, addresses the relationship between self and others, which is to say, citizenship. *O Cidadán* is built from four forms: Georgettes (lesbian love poems); catalogues of harm; documents; and aleatory poems that include banners, calculations, photos, and film scripts. The culmination of a decade of work, the poems selected from *O Cidadán* form the axis of *Planetary Noise*, as they condense the formal and thematic reverberations and modulations that exist across Moure's oeuvre.

Pillage Laud (1999, republished 2011) is in excess of the trilogy but related to it. It, too, probes the interface between lesbian textuality and (desiring) machine; in it, phrases were selected by hand (a lesbian sex-organ *par excellence*) from blocks of computer-generated sentences, and organized into poems assigned to a locale (conforming to N. Katherine Hayle's definition of "hypertext"). These "hi-toned obscurantist lesbo smut" poems, as Moure has impishly called them (*Wager* 145), are an investigation of "poetic form, [of] what the brain can understand emotionally from the poem as a whole (the macro level) even when in individual sentences (the micro level) semantic value is missing—there's no apparent sense" (145). Noise, here, functions as conduit for desire that reroutes attention and serves to "wrench open the circle of understanding" (148).

ATURUXOS CALADOS (*Galician Cycle*)
& AN ABSOLUTE CLAMOROUS DIN (*Ukrainian Cycle*)

The last two of Moure's poetic cycles represented in this volume, the Galician and the Ukrainian, are interconnected and represent over a decade of work from 2003 to 2015 and were both sparked at least in part by her *Sheep's Vigil by a Fervent Person: A Transelation of Alberto Caeiro / Fernando Pessoa's O Guardador de Rebanhos* (2001). Pessoa's use of heteronyms—or fully developed writing personas that have independent philosophies, biographies, and writing styles—began to influence Moure's own work during this period. The word "persona" is related to the mask, to the public face, and to the Latin *personare*, a word that contains the idea of "soundings" in "-sonare." Moure's polynyms (heteronyms, part-heteronyms, and escaped heteronyms, including those indicated by the altered spelling of her own name) can be usefully considered as "sonic masks"—as language sounding through the writer's body, resulting in characters with their own ideas and acts, separate from those of the author. In these cycles, theatre and noise poetics inform each other, and Moure, with her sonic masks, interrupts the turbulence of large-scale violence by deploying small-scale modes of listening.

When Italian Futurists F. T. Marinetti and Luigi Russolo celebrated the "art of noises," as Russolo called it, they did so by incorporating the onomatopoeic sounds of trench warfare, among other mechanical elements, into their idea of war on culture and women. Marinetti's "Manifesto of Futurism" of 1909 announces that: "We will glorify war—the world's only hygiene—militarism, patriotism, the destructive gesture of freedom-bringers, beautiful ideas worth dying for, and scorn for women . . . we will fight moralism, feminism, every opportunistic or utilitarian cowardice" (*Documents of 20th Century Art* 22). Russolo has a chapter in *The Art of Noises* celebrating sonic warfare called simply "The Noises of War" (49). These attitudes towards and approaches to war exemplify what Moure struggles against in these poetic cycles when she and Elisa Sampedrín (a Moure polynym) address the affective aftermath of twentieth-century genocides in Europe. The sonic masks provide only one among many techniques of listening that gently but tenaciously refuse the recklessness of the historical avant-garde and insist upon other noise poetics. Theatre and noise poetics join in Moure's later works in a dramaturgy that does not represent but that casts noise as an ethical threshold, an invitation to expand one's capacity to listen. In so doing, her theatre (or poetry as theatre) develops an art of memory based not so much on the intensity of the image, as are classical and medieval arts of memory, but on the porosity of external and internal borders and their amplification of sonic ambiguity. In this theatre, actors perform the work of listening and, as such, the traditional hierarchies of Western theatre begin to erode. Rather than looking to find and display artifacts of conflict for the audience, Moure's theatre acknowledges that conflict is already a condition of life in late capitalism, and instead she uses stagings to shift attention to other life conditions, if only briefly.

In both her Galician and Ukrainian cycles, Moure nomadically traverses social-historical, linguistic, and subjective spaces between urban Calgary and Montreal, rural Alberta, Galicia in Spain, and the Austro-Hungarian imperial province of Galicia, the east of which is today part of Ukraine. Moure has a personal connection to each of these places. Her father's grandfather emigrated from Spain's Galicia, one of the reasons that Moure chose to learn the Galician language (*Insecession* 44). Her mother was born in Velikye Hlibovychi, at the time in Poland, though it was once in Austro-Hungarian Galicia and lies presently in Ukraine. Both these places faced fratricidal and genocidal atrocity in the twentieth century. "There is a side of Europe we do not know and never learned of and still do not learn of . . . I still seek an ancestral cadence. A cadence of being and thought and harmony with trees" (*Insecession* 44). In approaching translation and exploring subjectivity (as cadence) in her poems, Moure gleaned cues from Clarice Lispector's use of *aproximação* and from the works of Fernando Pessoa's heteronyms. For Moure, *aproximação* means "to give [something] room and listen" (*My Beloved Wager* 180). She places this translational mode in relation to Fernando Pessoa's "amplification of identity" (*Wager* 180) to astonishing effect in her poems, stating that Pessoa does not fragment identity but "embraces it *excessively* in his heteronyms" (emphasis in original; *Wager* 181).

In the poems and texts of *Little Theatres* (2005), the initial book in the Galician series, we are introduced to Galician, a language of the extreme west of Europe, in a homage to water via the ingredients of her mother's national soup from the east of Europe, borscht. We then meet Elisa Sampedrín, a theatre theorist and director. Quotes from Sampedrín reject the gargantuan theatres of war and their deafening noise in English, in favor of little nicks of time and space and tiny noises in a language that has never been used to declare war, and where "[t]he protagonist . . . is most often language itself" (37). Sampedrín insists that "even the grass has a voice in little theatres" (40). In saying this, she argues with the idea that Peter Brook put forward in *The Empty Space* (1968) of "holy theatre," and leans toward Victor Shklovsky, who wrote in 1917: "And art exists that one may recover the sensation of life" (12). In this way, Sampedrín's theatre refuses ritual, including the ritual of character in relation to conflict.

In *O Cadoiro* (2007), the second book in the Galician cycle, Moure travels with books by Derrida on the archive and Foucault on the archaeology of knowledge as she tumbles into the medieval Iberian troubadour songbooks written in Galician-Portuguese. In her own poetic responses to these songbooks, Moure revels in the erotics of noise and noisy subjectivity, making claims for the radicality of lyric at a historical point when verse turned away from epic modes that lauded God or history to address instead a human individual, in a single person's articulated voice. The book is Moure's reply to those who would deride lyric, in particular some self-styled conceptualists who, unable to see the lyric as constructed, naturalize it in order to dismiss it, thus missing its transgressive power.

Just as *Pillage Laud* is a text in excess of the "Citizen Trilogy," there is now an interlude between Moure's Galician and Ukrainian cycles in the form of a clamorous collaboration of "resonant impostors" that unseats translation and any standard notion of its reliance on an original: *Expeditions of a Chimæra* (2009). This time a human collaborator, poet Oana Avasilichioaei, provides the occasion to deviate from the course. A book of pranks and reckless transits, of maps and the endless deferral of "arrival," it entangles subjectivity and performance in a fast-moving demonstration of translational modes of "passing." In so doing, it provides passage for Moure's work between Galicia and Ukraine.

In *O Resplandor* (2010), the first book in the Ukrainian cycle, translation, reading, friendship, death, and grieving are staged in different tempos. This book derives its title from a Galician word for light emanating from an object, like a halo; for Moure, it is a trope for reading, and for poetry. The optical phenomenon Moure evokes is that of blue light and its effect on our diurnal and nocturnal cycles and our perception of the passing of time. Moure uses this passage of time in the body to queer reading practice itself, as if reading can stop time, and translation reverse it. Elisa Sampedrín, by now considered not just a heteronym (though Moure considers her a polynym, i.e. not only heterogeneous to Moure but polyphonic in her own regard) but a Galician in her own right, reappears in *O Resplandor* in the mœbius strip of a contradiction: she is bent on translating the poems of Nichita Stănescu from Romanian—a language she does not speak—into English, because she wants to read them. In so doing, Sampedrín jostles at every turn with the unwanted presence in the book of Moure, who is seeking to locate Sampedrín in a time and place that already do not exist. In the second part of *O Resplandor*, Moure overtly borrows lines directly from an early version of Oana Avasilichioaei's translations of the Romanian poems of Paul Celan (published in 2015 in Avasilichioaei's *Limbinal*) and rearranges them, as she worries the noise of grief into a text(ile) within which to wrap the maternal body.

The Unmemntioable (2012), for its part, articulates a linguistic noise beyond any "unspeakable"; it is the noise, rather, of an interdiction, of what would perhaps be speakable, but is not mentionable. As Moure, in fulfillment of a promise made to her mother to return her ashes to her birthplace, appears in her mother's natal village in Ukraine, she comes face to face with two registers that trouble all process of memorialization: the legacy of the Holocaust, firstly, and then the legacies of the border changes and ethnic cleansings that by 1945 had brought to an end the multicultural communities in what had once been the east of the province of Galicia in the Austro-Hungarian Empire. In *The Unmemntioable*, E.M. the dreamer, on leaving Ukraine, again seeks the pragmatic E.S., Elisa Sampedrín, who desires only to be left alone in Bucharest to conduct her research into experience. E.S., in a fit of annoyance at E.M.'s stalking of her, steals E.M.'s jottings—which turn out to dwell on the infinite, to the disgust of E.S.—and then decides, as a kind of revenge, to use E.M. as her experimental subject. Whereas in *O Cidadán*, Moure employed the threshold of noise to question Augustine of Hippo's metaphysics of reading and the ideological limitations of his interpretations of "tolle lege" in the *Confessions*, in *The Unmemntioable*, Elisa Sampedrín worries the fabric of Ovid's poetry in trying to write poetry for Erín Moure. At the end of the book, the two subjectivities merge at an abandoned Art Nouveau or Secessionist style casino (what better way to meld experience and the infinite) at the edge of the Black Sea in Constanța, Romania, and the book ends by offering a wish for courage, in Galician, *coraxe*. Experience, it turns out, lies outside the book.

In *Kapusta* (2015), a bilingual poem in the form of a play, the staging of memory of the Holocaust via the grandmother and mother—who spent the war not in Ukraine but in rural Alberta—allows the indescribable noisiness of the "unmemntioable" to be spoken by staging it literally and figuratively, involving the reader or spectator in the responsibility to resist genocides, and thus ending the interdiction.

POLYRESONANCES (*Transborder Noise*),
POSTFACE, & Further Reading

Moure's work and its complexities and echoes can be read in conversation with the work of other major figures in North American poetry, poetics, and translation theory in the late twentieth and early twenty-first centuries. Incorporating philosophical quotations in the poem itself, and drawing from the major theoretical debates regarding language and subjectivity, Moure's work refuses easy distinctions between poetry and poetics, philosophical writing and poetic writing. I often read Moure's work as queer theory; her explicit engagement with the likes of Monique Wittig, Judith Butler, Donna Haraway, and other queer theorists leads to Moure's prescient work on queer affect theory, and the "queer art of failure." *O Cidadán* (2002) was published *before* Sarah Ahmed's *Queer Phenomenology* (2006) or Judith Halberstam's *The Queer Art of Failure* (2011), yet engages with these topics in a rigorous and wide-ranging way. Moure's work can also be read in conversation with the work of poets such as Phyllis Webb, Daphne Marlatt, Nicole Brossard, Lisa Robertson, Fred Wah, Roy Miki, M. NourbeSe Philip, Caroline Bergvall, Harryette Mullen, Bhanu Khapil, Rachel Blau Duplessis, Claudia Rankine, C.D. Wright, Andrés Ajens, Chus Pato, Oana Avasilichioaei, and Myung Mi Kim all of whom grapple with language and languages, and their relation to political and economic structures and to identity formation.

The final section of *Planetary Noise* is curated by Moure and offers the reader a window into her translations of other poets' work. These poems are not inserted in the other sections with her own work, as is often done in North American practice, as for Moure, translation is an opening of poetic culture in English to the work of others, not an absorption of it. Moure discusses her approach to translation in her Postface. A reader may also wish to consult the series of essays on translation that Moure published in *Jacket2* between 2012 and 2014—details are in the "Further Reading" list at the back of this volume, which includes a selected list of her own essays as well as essays on her work by others.

Moure is one of our most incorrigible contemporary poets. Her work is both challenging and a pleasure to read, and leads us beyond the dichotomies of schools and movements (conceptual, post-lyric, etc.) that tend to dominate contemporary North American poetics in English, to bring in other languages and connections. As I write this, with her books spread out on two-thirds of the sofa, I am reminded of the quickening feeling of reading and rereading each book, not only because they are so strange, but because their noise welcomes strangers unconditionally.

SHANNON MAGUIRE
Toronto and Sault Ste. Marie, Canada, July 2016

EARLY SIGNALS

First Cycle

from *Empire York Street* (1979)

february: turn toward spring

sunday, & the clutter
of words   black noise
that typewriter makes

outside. even the chirp
of sparrows has thawed, october
was the last i heard
of birds, & the songs.

two windows shattered
when wet bank of snow shifted
hard against them.
nothing in this place
is strong

between double panes, dead
insects. wasp, wire-legged
spider, beetle, luminous flies
all on their shoulders in dusty
sill

when the true thaw begins,
& the equinox they will awake,
struggle for air.
flip again onto damaged legs to devour
dirt from the ledge, patch crackt
glass w/ mucous & wait

then, as i sleep,
sparrow songs tight in my fists,
the insects will return, trek
w/ wings wet & folded
into my jaw; hooked legs
scarring my cheek
like a highway but not
that strong

& in the morning, spring, &
the fights, will have started
again

translation #1

between Ottawa & Edmonton
all the wires sputtered   *darling*
                            darling
before they wed
arrangements were made, changed, made
but not revoked
perhaps she boarded the train, leaving
what could not be jammed into suitcases
whatever past wouldn't fit
was discarded or rearranged
& ended anyhow in that eastern city
as she stood beside the airforce man
dressed in civvies, the war over, both of them
looking as tho they weren't quite ready
for the photographer;
that much is provable, if one wanted;
the whole scene ordinary or misplaced—
in the wrong season, Lent, there were
dispensations from bishops, then
they were married, drove to Québec
where he took pictures of her, hands folded
across her rings, sun at her head
in the prints her hair is eaten
completely white

today, twenty-nine years later, there is
no resolution, her daughter stands
somewhere in the prairie, beside the rails,
her own message stopped or
incomplete, telegraph wires still
singing   *darling*   in the same urgent tongue

photosynthesis

for Karen Shuster

you are old, or are you
young & unsure after all of the climate, the exact
necessity of particulars?
true, certain things can be verified:
you have a job, dental plan, an interest
in vacant houses, probably a motto.
you carry the right grudges, like to say you are
in control, & have no one look up
& state otherwise.
you have a schedule, & adhere to it, at least
in the mornings, if you get up.
after all, the universe has a limited cast
of characters:
& sometimes when you talk in a crowd, you hear
not yourself, but david, how he argued
for years before driving off the highway near lake louise.

how people give you what you never ask for, never want.
how a woman seen today on the street walks
w/ the peculiar gait you had five years ago.
yet then, when you stood in the light
beside the house & had david snap one picture,
& you gave it to me, now it is all i have, it won't answer
my questions, as you did, patiently.
all i can do, is peer, into the picture
& see how the light has changed you, you
are not so tall w/ the house leaning behind,
not so old, or covered w/ vines, yet
your face is white, its smile barely distinguished, your hands held nervous
together, like a chapel,
one leg slightly behind the other, you stand
bare feet hidden in the lawn, hesitant, smiling
having at last
no words for anything

Bird

The song builds its nest into the walls
Terrific noise of light   wakening,
released from dream.
Slow scrape of shoes, the day
shuffles back with its fingers & cut scalp, its wet
fussing kisses;
in its arms, a mess of food, an accordion,
the chairs toppled

Outside, the clouds'
grey cover shorn around the trees,
the last wet birds knock their heads
against the season,
their feathers smooth, chirping
    Love me, love me.
The walls sing, taxis spin past, lights glow;
a thin note holds us to the sky

After awhile, we learn to be alive, learn
how the day talks, its embrace muddies the corridor; & tells us
what brings white mist into the road
& thru the branches, birds
                        scarcely visible, singing

Full of seed & fragile wing-beat, blindly,
Their bright eyes free of us
This fallen year . . .

Subliminal Code

in memory, Dennis Wheeler

Across the screen, the white hands
of the dead man flutter, this is perfect
art; as he tells of terminals, sickness,
huge bodies possessing him,
the hands falter & rise, attending
his words—

In subliminal code the hands signal out
a window we do not see,
the camera's struck vision refuses it, or us,
watching:
as the hands call the buds on the trees
to burst open, the dead man
speaks of satire, disease, those who came
laughing at it; & how
the bodies became part of him, growing or
singing, in their outsized overcoats, their unwieldy clothes,
their tricks with minerals & wine.
He talks of losing
control, wanting the cures;
& of the day
he stopped believing in streets, taxis; now

his hands shudder white marks on the screen, the trees
burning around us, his hands enter the leaves, strain
to listen; they want to insist
something to a stranger at a crosswalk in Ottawa, L.A., Edmonton,
Vancouver, now
there are no more taxis;
his hands white leaves shimmering, push the cameras away,
finished, to a place
beside his ear, listen, on the bright screen
the hands of the dead man moving
spell

Why it is possible, it is, why
possible—
That the leaves burn so long in the trees,
they flicker & will not   go out, refusing this:

Philosophy of Language

A certain level of noise, the ear's false anguish, period.
She is reading a book, to herself, the
noise of this.
Huge rustling shakes the trees.
The windows fall open & lunge three storeys downward
in a pirouette, ready for suicide.
A man stands up before her,
for all his height he is no taller than her shoe.
It is the inventor of the hinge.
He wants her to praise him
for inventing it.
When she leans forward the noise of the book
blows him over.

He wants her to love him, that's all.
But he shuts her out, waving the god-damn
almighty
root of language.
For all his bellow, he is no more agile
than a verb.
For all his pirouette, he is no regeneration.
He is no earth & no simile.
When she leans her woman-being towards him, he is
no name.
She is her simple rustling, shakes him, utterly,
without syndical perfection,
without period

Jump over the Gate

I come home &
tell my mother I grew up.
I grew up! I say, & hug her.
Isn't it amazing! she says.
I go outside & open & slam
the door of the old refrigerator on the patio.
Our refrigerator!
Its round back like asthma, silent now,
a toque of snow over it.
Where did you come from? my mother says when I'm in.
I lay my mitts like two pages on the floor,
my boots dripping muddy smiles of water.
You! I say.

& she laughs. She's sitting at a high stool,
higher than the kitchen table,
paring an old soft cheese into a bowl.
I dip my hand in to taste.
It's good, I say.
Eat it on crackers! says my mother.

It bugs her most when I lean out the screen door
to call the dog out of the snow. Trix! I yell.
Puppy! I yell.
The dog is dead! my mother cries to me, but
I know she's still there in the yard.
Trix! I yell. We're going shopping!
Mom, I'm bringing the dog, I shout back to her.
Now the inside air is out, & vice versa,
it's cold.
Go ahead if that's what you like,
my mother sighs.
There should be a dog! I think.

Trix is with me & I let her run fast
& dip her head into the snow,
grabbing a big mouthful. She lopes ahead &
waits for me at the corners.
Cross! I yell.
& on the way back, I think:
if Trix were here she'd carry the package.
She liked to carry the package.
Trix! I yell for good measure.
Puppy! I yell for good measure.
When I get home, we both
jump over the gate.

You're back! my mother says.
There's really no Trix, I tell her;
& pass her the package, my boots scuffed with wet snow,
& pull the wool of my toque off my head.

I call her because I feel like it! I tell my mother.
I know! she says.
I know!

Lunge

All of a sudden you find out there isn't enough time.
You find out there was never enough time.
You find out you shouldn't have washed the dishes.

Over & over, so many dishes, the wet cloth, the spill
across the counter, window, bird out there
or not, the clean house, begin

& you find out you shouldn't have bought the clocks.
You shouldn't have bothered buying clocks.
You never had what they had to measure.

You leap up throw & them face-down into the trash.

There is not enough time to cry about this.
The pain in your back is very deep
& pointless.
You find out that all this time they said
you were part of the working class
there was no time.
The real working class in this country was always unemployed,
& you always had a job, the same one.

You find out there is no such thing as enough time
& still you don't have any of it.
You shouldn't have craved the arms of women.
You shouldn't have slept with men.
You shouldn't have dreamed *Philosophy*, or
the heart monitor screen in your apartment bedroom,
just like in Emergency.
It's all shit. Merde. This, & hey, & you others.

Time for the medicine. You fast cure. You fuck-up mad dog. You you. You lunge over the table. In mid-lunge. Going for the adrenalin again, going for keeps, prose, boots, the sandwich you couldn't eat, you bit & spit out, you thought it would make you sick again. Lunge for the dog's stale portion of sleep, your legs straight off the chair, your hair stuck out, the clatter of the chair falling backward, zone five, zone six, the sound of

Your arms make

Amicus, object,   referent

Points   of or-   der

Snow Door

Trying to remember, as if
The music, as if, as if

The music fell into my boots & I couldn't
wear them, couldn't feel.

The scent of orange behind the room's door... that note . . .
Physical space,   physical

space

Space between the window & its frame where the wind enters, chilling the
chairs. Dead flies between the panes, winter flies that come to life when they
warm up, but go stupid from the freezing, & can't remember flight exactly,
not exact enough, they topple on their backs & spin & buzz. Having forgotten
everything except that they used to fly, why can't they do it now. Too stupid
to know why they can't do it now.

Us, too,
who don't know we've been frozen, or if we have, &
if we know, don't ask questions.

I know I know.

My colleagues' mouths are opening above their male ties, spilling molecules
of air across the room, & I am this sad when I see it spilling, no one else
watches & I can't tell them, they are *serious*, & their jobs are filling up with
their bodies, their jobs are the shape of their bodies, I see their lives

fluttering, behind.

The woman I once knew
who reached her right hand into the glow & gripped the spoon,
flaming,
the physical reproduction of anguish
denial of physics
defiance   revenge

Snow door snow door snow door snow

Affectively, as if
The blizzard was over, we cut holes in the snowbanks,
our razor hearts burnished, our shovels raised up like sheet metal
As sentences, to make us   feel

A History of Vietnam & Central America
as Seen in the Paintings of Leon Golub,
Musée des beaux arts, Montréal, 1985

Several sections of this photograph are not visible.
Several sections have been repaired.
Several pieces of this canvas have been torn out
or covered over.
Several sections have been smeared.
If you turn around the photograph the result
is not the backs of heads.
The result of one painting sawn in three
is three paintings.
Several sections of this paragraph have been repaired.
Several sections have been forged with outside influence.
The woman holding the man's cock in the painting was also painted
by the man.
If the eye sees & the mouth describes.
If several sections of this photograph are not visible.
If the corn in the field winnowed new
teeth smiling
Several sanctions of this painting have been recently
restored
There is no speaking torn out & lifted says the president
There is no section of this painting you do not see

Several sections of this photograph have been torn out.
Several sections have been replaced.
Several parts of this poem are encoded to prevent theft
of language.
Several parts of this poem are encoded by theft,
to prevent language.
The mercenaries hold silver guns, they are throwing
the artist's body into the trunk of an American car.
Several pictures have not been taken.
Several times I have not stopped listing over.
The photograph gets smaller in the fingers.
When it is over we stand up & walk out, our breath fast,
uncreasing our knees

Pure Writing Is a Notion beyond the Pen

All of this an avoidance of the script:
the small turquoise shirt rolled up over the shoulders, the narrow
angle of sun in the yard, the body, the body,
oh, the body
with its view of the cold dew on the grass this morning, silver,
like a ring
Dreaming over & over of
women's madness, my mother's madness, the madness of
the neighbour woman shut up in High River,
where I was caught in a blizzard once, drifts choking the road & cars

until there is no anger any longer.
Until none of us is angry,
until our women's faces are the blindness of snow & refract light
until our house is so lit it has the sound of steel
until light becomes the absence of weight
& does not resemble us any longer

My brother out in his long yard stooped beside the haybine,
the thin swath of clover & timothy
drying in the sun, & the narrow muscle in his back, his head
completely vanished

into a place where there is no more childhood, just
the heat of August risen off New Holland equipment,
the connection   between   things & things,
the air hose & the tractor

air hose

tractor

In spite of us, the connection
between words, are words things, are they names of things,
the speed of light notwithstanding,
why do we go mad & forget everything, & be unable to speak of it,
as if: pure writing is a notion beyond the pen
she said, & held her head to keep the wind in,
& named it this

Unfurled & Dressy

Frontally speaking
I am facing up to my harbingers
I am wearing a small beam to stop from
measuring the sky
I am approaching my debits
with a voice left from the Elections
A yelp
The start of a cry

Frontally speaking I am leaning on the hugest boulder
by the wayside
in order to imprint the mountain on my ass
In order to jump into the abyss with my shoes named Kafka
In order to complete the fire escape of my marriage

Frontally speaking I am no more important
than the construction of a stadium
in the place where they refused to build
housing for the poor
I have inside me
no less sky than the sky

Frontally speaking my sadness wears another seven
beside your opportunity
It is unfurled & dressy
It is your voice which I am speaking over & over
because I like to hear you
inside my mouth
where I can touch our futures with my tongue
& throw down my names & embrace you
& forget which one of us I am
Frontally speaking
Frontally speaking

from The Acts

————1————

compression. To use a kind of compression, so compressed that the links between the image/phrases break down, but the whole poem still retains its connection.

inter-text. Using and repeating my own and others' earlier texts. Pulling the old poems thru the new, making the old lines a thread thru the eye of the words I am sewing. Sound & sense. The eeriness.

everyday event. Must take and use the everyday connection between things. Not talking a philosophical language. Watching terminology. Make the compression so hard that it functions as terminology, and I can just use the ordinary words in their street clothes.

physical body. Image of the whole physical body must always be there. Not truncated, not synecdoche, but the physical image speaking directly the entire body at once

The poems are called **Pure Reason**.

BECAUSE pure reason in the end is beyond all logic, and beyond the sign. Logic is just something imposed upon reason. It's one kind of connectedness, that creates points of conjunction and reference that may not be true, & may not have helped us much as human beings in the end (and certainly not as women). From where we are now.

PURE REASON is, of its essence, UNreasonable; it can't be itself reasoned or it wouldn't be pure reason. PURE REASON is the source of our reasonableness; our reasonableness (which may or may not be "reasonable") is its flaw. A leak. An uncontrolled space, at the edge. Where the so-called "purity" is already broken.

PURE REASON would be the source of Intelligibility, and Cause too. It must have to do with love, at its root. No matter how it is obliterated after that.

7

What is key to this desire: To have one's existence affirmed by others. Or, put oneself at risk forever (a panic at the cell's edge). Or is it affirmation, first, that then makes the risk possible? To bear it. The risk of, kissing her.

The embrace first, then the utterance.

What this need for affirmation meant before was having an existence affirmed by men. Knowing how they praise well what affirms their relation. They do not have to put themselves at risk, which women have always had to do, to exist, to speak, to have their existence affirmed by others.

What I had not spoken! The way she cried out because of my silence, & how I chose it, stubborn. My defense of necessity. Because my eyes and my whole body could see that the words and bodies of women were not listened to or affirmed.

We women listen so carefully to each other. The resurrection of the woman's body is of Kore, not the phallic king-dom. This affirmation is the true necessity. To inhabit freely the civic house of memory I am kept out of.

Oh!

8

What that surface is still haunts me. The people who move in the surface of the poem, becoming signs. Are they form or content.

They are not the real content. And in my loneliness, for days I am breathing brother air, my brothers outside throwing the football, the wall they are throwing it over is the huge gap between us. It is just air.

I think of the people who go around carrying the scars on their arms that they have made for themselves. It is defiance of the real. It is saying you can defy reality by mutilating your skin (that surface). As if your own physical matter is the place where you can leak outside of the real. It is a refusal of desire (at which point, do we not refuse memory too?).

The poet, instead, defies "real"-ity by writing it hard into the pages, building that surface (content), as a form wherein she makes her defiance visible. (The "real-" that women have never inhabited as whole beings: it has never been formed by our desire, Irigaray says.)

I want to write these things like *Unfurled & Dressy* that can't be torn apart by anybody, anywhere, or in the university. I want the overall sound to be one of making sense, but I don't want the inside of the poem to make sense of anything.

People who are making sense are just making me laugh, is all.

Is it impossible to conceptualize (in English) without using "the thing"? Our language that <u>objecti</u>fies TIME (i.e. the words "phase," "touch," which are really relations, not things) is one that supports easily the hegemony of "singleness," "individual power," "phallus." Its thingness before its motion. Because its motion is an ascent & descent. The female organs, that, Irigaray says, are "touching" before they are a thing. They can't be named as "things" without reduction. That are defined by their "relation."

It isn't that to change the weight and force of English will *necessarily* make women's speaking possible. But to move the force in any language, create a slippage, *even for a moment...* to decentre the "thing," unmask the relation...

What I brought back to poetry from my job was a stutter that replicated surfaces imperfectly, like the television screen with the vertical hold broken, no story possible, just the voices

heard again & again without image. Those dark voices. & I wrote, not into the book's heart, but out of fear, to make the image come back to me. Any image. My coat & shoes. My faint moving at the edge of the screen, blood in my head not moving but the room moving & the blood still... so that to move the force <u>for a moment</u> only <u>held</u> for that moment. (The word "held" a stillness, relational, not a motion...) (The word "moment" not a thing...) The preposition so relational it could not hold a <u>value</u>, & could hardly keep from vanishing.

I still believe in the relations & not the name. The symbol of relation. Hidden tensity of the verbs without tense. Because the past tense exists IN us speaking, or is not anywhere. We can speak of it separately because our language permits it. The future tense too. They do not exist outside our bodies! But in us as memory, & desire. Those <u>relations</u>.

& if we are to free our memories, our desires, we must refuse to <u>restrain</u> <u>ourselves</u>

CIVIC SIGNALS

A Noise Cycle

Hello to a Dog

Hello, dog. Heeeelllo, dog. Heelllo dog. Hello!
Mom I've said hello to this dog three times now,
it doesn't answer.
Hello dog.
Mom this dog doesn't answer.
Dog! Hello!
Mom! This dog doesn't answer. This dog! The dog I was saying
hello to. I said hello to it, three times.
I said hello to it more than three times.

Hi dog. Hellooo dog. Dog! I said hello to it three more times.
(Because perception is all we know of reality.
Because the surface & density of the words affect our
seeing, even if we don't believe.)
The dog has brown eyes black hair & when the sun hits, blue shoulders.

Because even buildings are held up by stresses in their
own structure.
Because of density.
Because the dog won't answer & no wonder.
Because the word has blue shoulders & when it laughs, so much envy.
Because of blue shoulders
Because of structure
Because of, "I have been in love"

The Jewel

The light air struck her, going in, the doorway
& its silver paper,
so festive

The light air struck her past the room's whirl & elevator
What was in her head, then,
likely

or not failed her, failed her here at last, in the office

The light room just an office
with its stained chair & terminal & fluorescent tube
the cup with its rhyme no

rime of coffee out of the brown machine where the red
light stares all day saying ononon ononon ononon
& nonono

So she dyed her hair red
So she dyed her hair red again when it faded
So she wore a red jacket
So she listened for the sound of her monthly blood
So she listened to her hair
So she listened to the soft fold of her jacket

The light over the desk, what can she do?
The phone speaking out of its cradle, what can she do?
The chair shaped physically for beauty, dulling her back, what can she do?
The green light notation of the screen, what can she do?

There are days we feel we are repeating, from some other time, we get
out of bed with the fish taste wet gills capsized boat of sleep
in our mouths & eyes rubbing as if the day has punctured
our careful wall, wall of dream, wall of physical memory
where the body knows itself, not gratuitous
Oh memory said Vasyl Stus, the sound of the Dnipro/
not gratuitous the dream punctured by the sound of alarm
& the hard faces of the wall, the wall, the other wall, four
walls of the room

These days I dream of the wet dawn smell of willows & the fishing rod
held high over the head, over ground cover, not
to be entangled,
the red & white jewel at the end of my line, dreaming its metal dream of
water, & me in the jacket too small
for the sweater I am wearing &
just this,
not being young or too young but being my age,
the age I am,
the wet dawn smell of the willows

My tongue like salt, not made for speaking
My tongue the colour of ice, what ice thinks before the storm
its crust clear in the dip of pavement
My eyes with their fine wrinkles, my eyes the eyes of my mother,
my tongue a bit of her knitting, where it came from,
her womb

I think of my father who went for years each morning to the office.
In his car.
Cutting the ice off the car's windows with a plastic handle.
Wearing a wool scarf.
Wearing a wool coat & handcuffs underneath that.

Wearing a belt, suspenders, glue, mahogany trimming, nails & screws,
a shirt with a package of cigarettes over the heart, a story of the air
force, *the time that, there was the time that, sometimes, in that time, in*
those times

Even, I think, in prison, far from
the town one knows, far from that territory & its river; in *Perm* in
Russia, in Kingston on the side of the lake, cold, invisible passage
beyond the wall,
the white ice & mouths of the carp,
their eyes sensing light & darkness,
it doesn't matter whose prison,
I think, one uses, for memory, the present tense

We are fishing in the cold river, emblem of the stream of blood leading
in & out of the heart, its loveliness manifest, the dawn
on the river, shallow, where the fish can't hide, where
in fact no one has caught fish,
who search the lonely pools of darkness & stay away from the dawn light
It hurts them
Dawn light
Red

The thyme in the mouth risen gorging the head full of sleep, I
wake up, am waking, my body alone naked house silent
around the wall, bed, drug of sleep, oh my drug
my hands warm tongue soft sheet in the mouth taste of thyme & silver
frost, on the window, light enters, the jewel light enters &
the darkness, begins

So she dyes her hair red
She wears her hair red
She wears the red coat of her blood
Soft tenderness
Soft smell of the thyme

What I miss is the absence of the image & tie to landscape, I, who am hugely
tied to the smell of yellow grasses & the sage, I, who am attracted to the dry
hills of the Peloponnesus, I walk out in them & press their smell to my face
& they smell crazily like the hills of Cochrane Alberta, my heart lives in that
dry corona & smell of sage

So her hair is red
So her hair is still red
So she runs her fingers dreaming thru her red hair
So her hair shudders
So she shudders
Her small, heart shudders
Her hand is red

My genitals covered, soft surface of the water red dawn light
the rod carried wall of sleep head of sleep corn porridge flat in the belly
flat cloth above genitals my genitals, my folded labia neat envelope &
warm put away fishing,
put away the green coat its memory of the pools where the rubber boots
lie, & tipped grocery carts, & grey slime from
the storm drains, street overflowed

put away your genitals
Gently

I am trying to think of the seven uses of the past tense.
Self-hatred, self-pity, guilt, fear of the body, separation from the
mother, trials in public court,

The office. I have to go to the office. Where I work. Today I have to get up &
go to the office. I have to comb my hair. I have to look like. I have to speak
without laughing. I have to wear my sweater. My hair. My hair arrayed how
how how. My light heart trips me & the darkness begins. I am not malevolent.
What will I do with my writing. I want to fail to understand notation. & the
sounds. Aphasia. I love you. My readers, I will be able to kiss you. The dryness
of my lips. I warn you. What we are given to understand. What we are given.
Begs the question. One question. So I can kiss you. The words kiss & question
unconnected until now

The Beauty of Furs

At lunch with the girls, the younger ones are talking about furs, & what looks good with certain hair colours. Red fox looks no good with my hair, says one. White fox looks snobbish, beautiful but snobbish, says another one. They talk about the pronunciation of coyote. I think of my brother catching muskrat. I think of pushing the drown-set into the weeds, the freezing water of the Elbow, the brown banks & snow we lived with, soft smell of aspen buds not yet coming out of the trees, & us in our nylon coats in the backyards of Elbow Park Estates, practically downtown, trapping. *Coy-oh-tea*, the women say. In some places they say *Ky-oot* or *Ky-oht*, I say, thinking of the country where my brother now lives, the moan of coyotes unseen, calling the night sky. & me caught in the drown-set so deeply, my breath snuffled for years. & then it comes. They are talking about the beauty of furs, and how so-and-so's family is in the business. I remember, I say, I remember my mother had a muskrat coat, & when she wore it & you grabbed her too hard by the arm, fur came out. Eileen, fifteen years older than me, starts to laugh, & puts her hand on my shoulder, laughing. We both start laughing. I start to explain to her that it was old; my mother wore it to church on Sunday & got upset if we grabbed her arm. We're laughing so hard, now the young ones are looking at us, together we are laughing, in our house there was a beaver coat like that, Eileen said, then suddenly we are crying, crying for those fur coats & the pride of our mothers, our mothers' pride, smell of the coat at church on Sunday, smell of the river, & us so small, our hair wet, kneeling in that smell of fur beside our mothers

The Beauty of Furs: A Site Glossary

Later you realize it is a poem about being born, the smell of the fur is your mother birthing you & your hair is wet not slicked back but from the wetness of womb, the fur coat the hugest fur of your mother the cunt of your mother from which you have emerged & you cower in this smell. The fur coat the sex of women reduced to decoration, & the womb the place of birth becomes the church in which you are standing, the womb reduced to decoration, where women are decoration, where the failure of decoration is the humiliation of women, to wear these coats, these emblems of their own bodies, in church on Sunday, children beside them. The church now the place of birth & rebirth, they say *redemption*, everyone knows what this signifies & the mother is trying to pay attention, all the mothers, my mother, & we are children, I am children, a child with wet hair cowlick slicked down perfect, no humiliation, the site still charged with the smell of the river, the coat smell of the river, smell of the birth canal, caught in the drown-set is to be stopped from being born, is to be clenched in the water unable to breathe or see the night sky, the *coyohts* calling me upward, as if in these circumstances, so small beside my mother, I could be born now, but cannot, can I, because we are inside this hugest womb which has already denied us, in which we are decoration, in which men wear dresses & do the cooking, & the slicked hair is not the wet hair of birth but the hair of decoration, as if I could be born now, I am born, my snout warm smelling the wet earth of my mother's fur

Seebe

The mind's assumptive power
The assumptive power of the mind over the mind
The carrying of spit upward to the mouth on the end of a knife
this incredible spillage,

release of the river behind the dam at Seebe, recoil of water
rushing the gorge, where we have stood, our lines
taut connection between us & the water's surface, our blastular memory,
(t)autological

who we are, now, the spaces between words where time leaks out
& we are finished, finished, gone old;
the table of food finished & the guests left, & the spillage of glasses, &
our shirts empty, empty,

They say what saves the bones is weight-bearing exercise
except for the carrying of children
Which is our namesake,
which is what we do, naming

children,
taking their torsos in & out of the uterine wall
then carrying them, lifting
the weight of the small boy up from the side of the rails
& running toward the train, stopped for us, his leg soft with blood
spattered my uniform, his leg not broken, just torn a bit at the skin,

This spillage, rusted gates pulled upward
to release the downstream blood
The mind's assumptive power of the Bow at Seebe
Carrying the boy to the conductor & then running back for the
kit, sunlit, "we hit a cow" they said in the lounge car afterward,
& me lifting the boy up from the dam where he was fishing,
the bridge where the whitefish run among the planted trout at Seebe

lifting him upward, his Nakoda face & bone weariness, watching me
white woman from the train taking him upward
into the vast, vast emptiness

Actually he was in the weeds
Actually he was nested hurt leg red in the weeds beside the train
so as not to be found again, got that?
All the tourists on the dam fishing sunlit maybe first hot weekend of summer,
delirium, delirium, trout dreams of the uterine memory, pulled upward on
the thin lines, water running high into the reservoir, oh Bow, oh hotness,

we hit a cow, they said

The sudden yet soft emergency braking, pulling the cars up expert not too hard, we hit a cow they said in the curved light of the lounge at the end of it, & breaking out the side door lifting the green box, knowing nothing, knowing the sunlit heat on the back of the blue uniform, running down the right of way, the body not used to it yet, this gravelled running, the hot smell of spruce & light air of curious voices, the boys on the bridge having run, then; not knowing what would be found there, thinking of what to do in the bright run in the sun,

1) check breathing if you can find the mouth,
2) stop the bleeding,
3) immobilize fractures,

thinking the second step, going over it in the mind, so that when you look at someone completely bloody you see blood only where it is moving, it is the assumptive power of the mind, the mind over the mind, the deconstructive power of the human body, to take this, outward

He was in the weeds. & scared. He looked up soft at me. Hey, I say. You're okay. He was hiding from me. I could see him. & ignored his hiding. Dropped the kit & bent over the torn leg. Blood, that's all. Only one leg. The foot aligned well with the rest, okay, feeling up & down the bone, no, okay, just torn up & bleeding where? Here. Bleeding here. Okay. Lifting him up then & running carrying him back up to the train, the blue cars creaking, conductor, wait

give him up

& run back, the green kit just sitting tipped on the right of way, beside those weeds, grab it & run back, daring to look around at the trees & warm smell forest finally, jump back into the cars, we're off then

The poem has fallen apart into mere description.

It is years later, thinking of the minds assumptive power and remembering the train hitting the boy at Seebe, Alberta & how I went out to get him. Here we have only my assumptions, only the arrogance of Erín Moure made into the poem; in the course of history, which is description, the boy is mute. We have no way of entering into his images now. The description, even if questioned, portrays the arrogance of the author. In all claims to the story, there is muteness. The writer as witness, speaking the stories, is a lie, a liberal bourgeois lie. Because the speech is the writer's speech, and each word of the writer robs the witnessed of their own voice, muting them.

Lifting him up, bone weary, taking him
into the vast, vast emptiness.

Excess

Standing in the snow below your window covered with
flowers the light in your frame the trees bare & snow fallen
wet on the walk & the flowers & these lines in my head
hating the romantic impulse because it leaks & the sentence
goes on & on excessive I don't want it to end the blank
space beyond the period hurts I want everything to occur
before it & you don't hear me & the snow is excess & the
flowers are excess
& as for me standing here

what am I writing

this too is excess

This too is excess this giving
birth to *our fathers* who taught us the normal
home explosive or shunted off not feeling
& now for me you are explosive
& I for you shunt you off not feeling
my father
your father
we have given birth to each other's homes
excessive
the static

Two women who adore their fathers get along
their lips folded fingers talking
shift on the restaurant chairs &
call for wine
& the ones who carry within them instead
the huge punitive seed of the mother
with its bowed colicky flower
folded up
We balance the weight of our lives
separate &
"Fond of each other"

The immeasurable tendency of the line veers
toward the centre
The jumble of the body follows: liver pancreas kidneys
in that hugest organ: the skin
the organ our fetish craves

So much it is the trace of our aging
the remnant of its markings on the hands & eyes
makes
the entire body visible, those years, too, like all else
in the skin's design, our first kiss is still there
Excessible

An entropic order. Say "en)tripic horde or"
The tendency toward the centre breaks down
the fucking organizm
A synecdoche
where "the whoel" stands now

for "the part of"
The whoel being an excess,
unpresentable

Huse some images, she says, standing up
with that beautiful fist's grip on the beer, the rat
waving from the window, that rat
in the bad dream, her fist's grip on the beer
standing or that other woman gone to Les Antilles
& one woman not talking to & you in the wrinkled
coat holding a fork meat rice the people passing
outside in the darkening presence women on the street
strolling *are min arm*

I tell you the predominant speech is the cure for
the excess of publishing the head pulls thru itself
daily we can't slice it, use some images she says she
asks for it, she does, standing up
with that beautiful fist's grip on the beer, the rat
waving from the window, its pretty
hand, its
pretty nice hand or

The presence of our fathers
Between us, the explosible or
the fear of being shunted off unfelt
The father's stories: *no ideas but in things*

with our preponderant guilt
deep in us, swimming as if
we are not quite yet crowned
out of the folded flower
turning down to up & breathing the first room of
oxygen & carbon
we walk near each other, wearing
the flecked distance of her womb

(it was not our fathers but we
who made in her the hugest
sensation

We are first of all
an excess then
the place at which the line disturbs
the skin
that organ folded
turned inside out to make us

our fingers
perfect replicas of
who we *always already* are

& if the disturbance echoes as a kind of
romance bothering you & haunting my
skin Romance waiting outside your window
my head bowed & hair visible,
oh can't I, won't you the huge sigh of
memory
as if the disturbance so great the static now reaches
the front of the house, the tree still
the sidewalk still the stone front of the house built in
St. Louis du Mile-End annexed that year to Montréal
built stone disturbance here I tell you
snow & flowers
snow & flowers
as if (no) room in the heart for this excess of feeling the
love
that makes us long for
our self-made loneliness, the "I am" of that,
the "she who thinks" of that, the

To give the proper names to each syllable, identify
the phonic phoric (eU)static, ex)stasic physical
presence, the head, the bone inside the ear, we are
speaking as if
we are already someone
there is no mistaking us

Use some images she insisted holding
her hand up, carrying the beer the Lotus Hotel
in 1982, there an image alright we
can be lesbians now
it's already alright, the image she calls for,
covers up the unaccountable
excess

Romance

Romance itself embedded in the referent(ial)
sign, the sign "beer" meaning round tables dark &
the agonic bleat of women's voices
The desire for lyric: to shut down & modify the excessible
Lyric noise (Not romance but the failure
of the sign to mean, we're lost in it, not forest but the
sign) or what the hell the lesbo-ex-machina:
if the ending fails, send them to bed

(& for those who crave the image, sensible:
"their arms touch each other"
"she jumps up & kisses her"
What more do you want from me.
There is no excess unbound by the image.
"She wakes up beside her in the flowers & snow"

from *Sheepish Beauty, Civilian Love* (1992)

Song of a Murmur*

Having been satisfied with the weight of
silver,
having measured with a small spoon the portion
of manganese in the internal heart,
having done this,
having done these things, & more,
having seen to the softest tears of the vagina,
the sicknesses of the seed which our children have become
because

it is so small living inside of this seed
inside of this air
inside of this latitude of the air
where the air is,

inside of this seed.

—

Having been satisfied with the measurement of the bank
accounting of the rich, who do not recognize us
in these forbidden sweaters,
in these sweaters we have been forbidden,
our mouths above their knitted necks & shoulders speaking

like graffiti on old bridges
this "like" making sure of the intelligible insistence
of the similar, the architecture of analogy that functions
in the head as thought
that we think "thought"
in thinking

—

because at first, when I was young, I suffered so
from the cranial dichotomy
I wanted mirth & toast, & accepted to remember
thoroughly
everything
in the permitted strength of original comparison

& no other way
& not to listen to the crying of the seed
where so many of us are living

—

it is cramped space & at night we are kept awake

by the internal heart we have remembered
the deafening splinter in the soil
that will grow into a tree
before we are free of it
By which its myocardial insufficiency, oh
reader

—

does your mitral valve flutter?
if so, are you ready to obey it?
three straws for the manganese of your shoulder?
your bank account?
are you satisfied with the weight of it?

if so, are you ready to drop your drawers, sir?

To DM, SH, AL and others it may concern: *This is a complex poem whose socio-political implications deserve deciphering.*

---

*What the murmur is singing is that the capitalist system, based as it is on individualism and individual greed, separating human beings, stinks.**

Note to people who have difficulty laughing at themselves: the above note explains nothing and is a JOKE. You may well ask: WHAT socio-political implications? It is clear that the poem doesn't have any. Ideology and art don't mix.*

In some schools, jokes are not allowed in poems. And the poet must be very polite, politer than this one, who ends her poem as if to say: get fucked or get your ass kicked. What business is it of hers to adopt this superior tone, appropriate for a seasoned politician, not for a respected artist?*

****However, please remember it is the murmur who is singing this. The poet is only an observer, a private individual, and the murmur is an act of the imagination.

NOISE RISES

Citizen Trilogy + Pillage Laud

from Search Procedures, or Lake This

Interpretative relax. Hormone
exigence parfois aimerait
cut-up laughing. You're
symbolise rien coulait ce que
physis empathetic impetus of
Honte. Amertume légère de son
madness, dance of spout lineal
fusion du possible. Espérons
interpretive gleam. Side view
boîte ouvrante très proche à
collaborative drive. Edge visible
ôtez le « je ». Interpellant
literal land layer, adverbial
poudre, saurons donc respirer

"literal land layer," as if layered in the head, words lined by dint of

Institutive angular just. Cooperate autant que les lésions de lumière Alexandria. Institutic grammar to Plancher balayé direct. Hésitations epidermal suggest. Relative amnesiac du rêve historique. Gestes de fines endeavour. Palliative care, festered restez indemne. Fenêtre ouvrante sur shared archway. Remedial glance at Son tonal. « Salbutamol » dorénavant phraseologue plays an indicative role. « Tu gares ton auto. » Intercollant. Top glue. Slow musical note of*

"interpretation," each layer oscillating, ignites cortical screens or paths

*« Lente musique de »

Obelisk nature but we're wowed, eh. To touch
ce beau monde. Malaise conduisant par-dessus
in granitic lesion, deposited unequally on terrain
mal interpreté. La lumière symbolise une détente
singularly absent, leaking, miscreant device
au paysage littoral. Mots anglais bien compris
"outa here." Don't laugh, then. Arms flexibly
livrés de toute peur. Diffraction irrémédiable.
Absolute cynicism at radar pace, detectable

L'être « femme », il faut dire « ça »

unavailable to the expulsive reader who dismisses "absolute" a piece

Tomorrow. Use of this word "wick ears"
ci-haut mentionné. Chaleur de chez nous
point de repère. The film projected at
elles s'extasent riantes élèvant leurs
verbal pneumae. Inflammatory ruse
illogique, sont des brigandes de la rue
some introductory collusion evident
vagues froides de la mer. Partout
dawn. Pale joints of the body, spiritus
portent les vestons de nylon, c'est-à-dire
sound "Mont Royal" nocturnal hum of
demeurons ici, facilement, sa dédicace
diminished. Her eyes.
résolue

where so little "actually" fits together, there is no palpable image or whole

La saute de mémoire. Devant l'expiration
nominal. Histrionic, I said, not hyst-

or the "whole" is an elaborate leap of memory, of inner noise &

The Notification of Birches

: Customs

for Gail

I am thinking about *the fact of essences*
played out in the theatre of disbelief

There is a sense in which poetry cannot tell
the truth about anything

Except to say
"before us there is a birch forest"

As opposed to prose
where there are truly essences

Persons, repositories of belief
without whom the rest of us are nothing

we stand absolved

the birch forest astounds us who are accustomed
to "aspens"

the white trunks of the "bouleau" in autumn
out there

or deer

: Sense

There is a sense in which
poetry is not the notification of anything

abrupt

the acknowledgement of peaceable discontinuity
in our lives

a storm of which is remaindered
grass sticking out of it
the beach houses held shut with plywood

over which, the layers of the wind
painted with a thick brush-stroke

(how can we exceed this with werdtsz)

: Coats

In particular, the coats we drape to make the cold turn back
wordless

out there with the constellation Orion
who is falling slowly, shield downward

where does the cold go when we do not let it into our bodies
our small wings we could have grown & failed

There is a sense in which it is no good to
talk so clearly about a "life" in poetry

or the way it feels writing this
(should I say so?)

Those wings withered & small in the space under the arm
Between this arm & the central body

The furnace
or pen

Talk instead about the constellation tipping slightly
Talk instead about the line of expressiveness

: Economy

If you held a pen under the arm to read the temperature
of the next strophe

A periodical leafed through & abandoned against a tree
is "garbage" but becomes us

Women in the workforce are forces of immediate expression
of the economic foundation of existence

of self
the economy of being

there is a sense in which poetry fails to exercise
the faculties fully

due to the lull in the head brought on by tiredness
(birches represent "amazement" here)

: Language

Or the birches represent amazement
having been swept forward

& up
Out of the imagined river

legally blind or incapacitated & waiting for a chair
the essence of "being"

Use-value, usefulness are in the saying
we do not know this or anything otherwise

or still

They turned us upside down & shook us
held us up like fish

we knew then there is a "world of spaces"
moral value

we came from the culture of fishes beforehand
the teeming at certain rocks excites us truly

thought is sediment, laid down, beautiful

a r yp al oï

The Splendour

1

Is it rigour or is it patchwork
Riding, alone, the engine of economy

A splendour
(or is it)

Trying to be as curious
Trying to forge an upset frame of reference
Pulling the window thru the door,
her blue sweater gradually emerges
or rocks where she had crossed

the Elbow River
A splendour (is it)
Following "Louise's" laugh
An economic dwelling where we all have been spilled or tarnished

Alone, but such
I connote her arm where once no art was possible
A true life

we have been seeking
is it seekable

or "stake in"

2

What it is, we wait
as once we did
Await the father's anger which we knew as love
Tools & soil inhabit us

(it is so difficult not to be bitter
as such
Communicáte or icon, a slick rock she once did slip on
in the Colorado River, falling)

Because it is such difficulty names us...
I "admit"

3

A zone where tremors do inhabit
We are at ease here
Our heart shocks us every moment

A respite is what we long for
To be honest
I remain

---

* imagine

4

Where keys of doors & doors of poetry
An insistent anecdote brings up her smile
Last seen in June (it is November)

As such, time passes
we refuse it
Kale, mimosa, milk & resin

Time passes
Poems recuperate, but do not solve
We refuse it

do not obey
or chastise

pulsate

5

The realm here is
irremediable

Thus in my act I do remember
what is memory
If not

aberrant splendour

6

I insist upon (falling into the fall or river, shoes wet)

to pulsate*

from Calor

> *Must our fear of sign-systems, and therefore, our investment in*
> *them, be still so immense that we search for these pure positions?*
> JEAN-FRANÇOIS LYOTARD, Libidinal Economy

What is "set in motion"?
What "is cured"?
If so, "what is a remark"?
& what is justly "evident"?
Who "freaked out"?
Which woman "had a bird"?
Which held a blue teléfono *en el ruido de la calle*?
Who withstood hail?
Who watched at the moorish embellishment of stone?
Which one ordered the 3rd bottle between 2 on c/ Elvira?

Whose reason "stank"?
Whose version was missing a forehead?
"Who is Andalusian"?
Who "stuck her neck out"?
Who, because?
Who "felt grief"?
Whose heart was a "cherish, aimless girl"?

For whom did the name "cohabitate"?
Lying in the narrow room over the cut wood.
For whose heart, grazing her shoulder?
For whose light jaw, its touch of grain on that tangled shoulder?

Where faith was?
Where the odious was a syllable?

Who painted.
Whose fear tore out, leaving the gauze.
Whose veil vanquished.
Whose furious gaze bore no answer?
Who shuddered in such, "in such" a wind?
Whose "wound" bore cause?
Whose syllable met "who"?

I love you. A use? Te quiero.
Whose "was" the Atlantic storm? Who brought rain?
Who did we "ever know" "enough" of?
Whose crater vanquished?
Whose "seemed"?

Whose arroyo winked its pellicule?
Who was there at noon, holding the fresh gauze
on the plaza where the rain spattered
on the book with the cloth-bound cover
on the cobble where the cortical gruel of the accident finally vanished

Because it rained
Because its gutter was a Tuesday's worn endeavour
A microchromatica of the blood
A treasure of sane belongings
An object of doubt...

Whose tome fenestrated daylight?
Whose wore, for awhile, a rough sheen?
Whose surface was "calm"?
A horse intruded.
Whose declaration "mattered"?
A gate of doors.
Whose dream vanished?
Whose dream stuttered an achey name?
A dog intruded.
A clam.

An absolute sonorousness
sinew of her shoulder.
Jerks in sleeping.
Sinew the noise of water, a fountain at dusk lit up
Confabulate "a body" enter.
Fain.

(Not a gate or horizon.
Not a cleft we have known.
Not a "spirited girl". This she was lent only for a moment. This she borrowed.
This a swank gauze she could not honour or defend. This a sorrow's touch of
so much "human feeling". This the name of water out of "some" fountains. This
a sentence containing "those blousy men". This a fragrance of lent oranges.
Her shoulder. This

her shoulder? Her shoulder. A leaning, *con su permiso*. That once. It was set
in motion. No one of us had eleven. No "once" of us was cured.)

There was a cold
In which

A line of water across the chest risen
(dream)

Impetuate, or
Impetuates

Orthograph you cherish, a hand her
Of doubt importance

Her imbroglio the winnowing of ever
Does establish

An imbroglio, ever
she does repeatedly declare

to no cold end
Admonish wit, at wit's end, where "wit" is

from *O Cidadán* (2002)

"An ailing nationalism can only recover through the force of abstraction."
FERNANDO VALLESPÍN, El País, 15 January 2001

"When pushed to the wall, art is too slow."
LISA ROBERTSON, "Thursday," *The Weather*

Georgette

Georgette thou burstest my deafness
woe to the prosperities of the world

because I am not yet full of thee I am but a burthen
to myself

Thou breathedst odours, and I drew in breath and
did pant for thee, I tasted and did hunger, where thou
hast touchedst me I did burn
for peace

time's subject motional and "form"
a code of vinyl
bar's emphasis

there yet live in my memory the images of such things

the hearse upon a station
a cross upon a fear
an insigne upon a hearth

folio
::::::::::
adore

document15 (differential plane)

It is citizenship's *acts* I dream of, acts not constrained or dilated by *nation*, especially as *nation-state* and its 19th c. model of sovereignty. Rather, *acts* as movements or gestures across a differential plane, not tied solely to ideology's (history's) rank function. But how to articulate this without invoking transcendent "citizens" as if Platonic "ideas"? What seed autonomy will speak dress? This "differential plane" also a wheel whose spokes bend yet still it rolls. Captain Paul Grüninger in 1938 at St. Gallen, physically a prosthetic application of "Swiss border," altered 3600 passports to permit Austrian Jews entry to his country. Forgery and insubordination, his *délits d'hospitalité*. To make one's own inviolable seam permeable: this act a citizen's act. Or Christoph Meili, "former" bank guard, who took Nazi-era documents from the shredder, Switzerland, 1997. "After having considered other options, he finally decided that the career of a knight errant would be the most rewarding, intellectually and morally." "How can God meet us face to face, *till we have faces?*"[1]

The Basque philosopher Unamuno saying that what led Juan Teresa Ignatio to "mysticism" was the perception of *an intolerable disparity between the hugeness of their desire and the smallness of reality.* Alonso Quijano, who "obstinately refused to adjust the hugeness of his desire." The matter of density between an aspect and a principle, manner's vocabulary. Could her arm serve the universe? Unless the café of men churned a decade, how were the vacations of panic going? Have they extended? What have I charged?

We are your forests. We stopped you.
Gutter inimical to fear.

Or acting across a surface.
Itself hurt.

Women were gathering.
Oil's testimony, vigour

In S. Leys, "Imitation of our Lord Don Quixote," NYRB 11.06.98, quoting C.S. Lewis. In '71 on Swiss TV (a year before he died), G. said: "My conscience told me that I could not, and would not, send them back." The Swiss government finally pardoned him in 1995.

document22 (wound throat)

How is *o cidadán* to get out of "citizen" expressed as "essence" (as in Augustine's hearing of the voice)? So as to see sovereignty of person or nation as other than stemming (historicized) from this essence?

To disturb "the subject" as "essence" is also to disturb *the citizen* as a figure banking on that essence. And yet it's true that the citizen can't *be* a pure exteriority.

The interiority (subject-relation) of the citizen is a disturbance/turn, rather than a strict identity. But this is what makes it beautiful! *Moi fermosa.* "After I am a clarinet, you can dream." "Won't velvet rust?"

The wound throat possibly appeared

(the screen of affection is sleeping)

document32 (inviolable)

When "my language" <u>fails</u>, only then can we detect signals that harken to a porosity of borders or lability of zones... (across the entire electromagnetic spectrum, not just the visual. as in *planetary noise*)

But first we have to suspend our need to see "identity" itself as saturate signal (obliterating all "noise"), following Lispector

into a "not-yet"—

How a woman wanting to write can be a *territorial* impossibility. And *reading* (bodies or others) is itself always a kind of weak signal communication, a process of tapping signals that scarcely rise off the natural noise floor.

(the noise generated by a system within itself)

Think of Ingeborg Bachmann in her hotel rooms. Her unsettled acts were noise's fissures. To see her as citizen is indeed to know *citizen* as repository of harm, where harm is gendered too. Myths of violability, inviolability, volatility, utility, lability played out. In wars, women are territories, and territories are *lieux de punition*.

A César o que é de César. *(Bachmann in Rome.)*

"to interdepend" (Clarice says)

Thus body/body image and the city, for the city or citizen-relation is itself spatial. And is thus also psychically invested. Space begs time's notion (n) and need, a history.

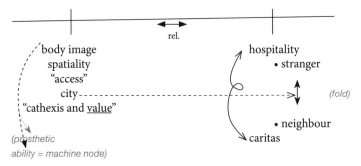

The symptomatology of the accent invades writing.... (D *MO* or *PO*)
"*The secret harmony of disharmony: I don't want what is already made but what is tortuously in the making.*" (Lispector, *AV*)
"The language called maternal is never purely natural, nor proper, nor inhabitable." (D)
And that <u>lability of meaning</u> means sexual organs might be *invested in* or *migrate to* any region of the body, "they don't have to be cathected genitally" (cf. Grosz) [i.e. her right ear]: this runs parallel to Derrida's symptomatology of the accent. An accent too is labile, and sexual cathect is also *accent*. Funny thing is: an organ could also, then, be cathected outside the body-"proper" so that the body-"cognizant" oversteps the body-"proper" at any given time. Which <u>creates</u> time, by *pushing space sideways.**

**which means the "originary space" (i.e. soil) is a* ~~pathetic~~ *fallacy?*
"spatiality" "access" "value" => are these cathected differently for women?

Georgette

What is my proper self
philanderer of griefs⁻

malestar divinity
in the integrity of "a situation"

- - - -

we who have from the start
ignored being

thinking it
a separation from anatomy

but this is blaspheme's code

to become architect   endeavour's touch
is possible's fond connect

where your ankle touched my shoulder
the cord shudders in the spine
                                        being vertebral
                                        to a crouch or all

                                        not veneer

⁻*thus hard to register*

document37 (no tempo das fronteiras)

In the hospital certain organs are removed, a kidney, thyroid: disease, transplant, vocation. Outside and inside: two types of mechanics visible. One spurts upward. Soul? Race?

To situate in a place. Declare creates us. Occasions are my composers.

What does it mean for the *border* if, in determining the subject, its "signification is not a founding act, but rather a regulated process of repetitions that both conceals itself and enforces its rules precisely through the production of substantializing effects"? (Butler, GT) With agency located in the possibility of variation on that repetition.

Is citizenship, too, that agency? Not "origin" but the signal that traverses or imbibes, breaks...

Butler calls "boundary" an effect, an apparent stabilization in "matter" of what is actually a materializing process, not matter itself. If so, then when a materializing process is hit by influences *slightly out of step*, the boundary becomes porous. Membrane into the head. *"For three weeks, [de Sousa Mendes] worked day and night, signing papers for anyone who needed them, in his office and in his car."*

O reader.

I too have lived reason's difficulty. "To touch ceaselessly on the confines of the world" (N). My demand was a sound inside pleasure. Being "as such." Not that routine of hurt *palabra.*

where the signal itself (Hegel) becomes "noise" and it is other potentials closer to the threshold we are seeking. A porticle. Aporetic. Leakages across a line. Bis.
De Sousa Mendes, Portuguese consul-general in 1940 in Bordeaux, France, issued 30,000 visas to refugee Jews, admitting them to Portugal in direct defiance of instructions. He was recalled to Lisbon, forcibly retired, denied full pension, and died in 1954, destitute. He was not officially rehabilitated by Portugal until 1988.

~~sovereign body39~~ (vis-à-vis)

What if we listen then to the noise and not the signal?
tor = tower
blé = wheat

visi (vis-à-vis) = a relation, also: isi – a certain symmetry of i's around a
curved channel.
v = the hand   (man
                      mão)
                       a
                       ã

                 certain alphabetic letters.

O cidadán is not the person subject to rules/laws, who then carries out this
subjection ("the sovereign") but "one who does not accept the gap" and...

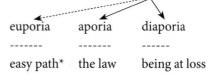

     euporia   aporia   diaporia
     -------   -------   ------
     easy path*   the law   being at loss

...therefore one who acts differently. (Quichotte)

*always dreamed of, always missing

document40 (vocais abertas)

A voice, his children reported, had told de Sousa Mendes what his conduct should be. *Quixoteridade*. To *conduct* a leakage out of originary language, out of the monolingualism in one's own language that would keep boundaries pure.

Tolle lege.

"Face is an experiment against prayers." Further: Lévinas's take on "hospitality" is one that interrupts interiorization/incorporation of an other, is instead a space of interruptibility or leakage where there is no claim to totality. The one welcoming the visitor is already in the visitor's debt, for visi-tor is also visi-ble, brings the visible into being. *Tor and blé.*

Tor y trigo.   *Isthmus.*

Which honours "the space between" and does not produce a subject/object relation; both faces remain present unto each other. Time's heteronomy. Buber's "I/Thou." Here Hegelian dialectic (in its popular sense) does not operate. As in the threshold environment of weak signal communication, what we face/hear is present only within the noise generated by the planet's surface, the solar relation, the system of detection in itself. Here noise is temperature and mapping and we are not seeking "strong signal"

We are listening to something much quieter (our debt fierce opening

"as vocais multiplicadas"

To touch ceaselessly on the confines of the world...

Sixteenth Catalogue of the Sorbas of Harms

We rode out the proofs of industry.
There was a window of time to do so.
Because 18 Texas Rangers died, the great America (Albright)
turned its back on the slaughter of
800,000.
Did we forget?
What did we forget? Do the Spanish "dream"?

The bus crossed the terrible dry hill of Sorbas.*

*Anybody knows there is no hill at Sorbas.

--- -- --- -- --- -- --- -- --- -- --- -- --- -- --- -- --- -- --- -- --- -- --- -- ---

But we have photographs of this hill! The fabrication by the media in 1914
of atrocities. Coverup of the human meats. Or: the French in 1942 who *did
not know* the fate of the Jews, when some were committing suicide to elude
"the transports." The NYRB piece⁻ that does not seem to notice (Papon
trial) that separating citizens because they are Jews and "deporting" them
to work on "farms in Poland" is already a crime.

800,000 dead in Rwanda in these recent years.

"Farms in Poland."

If I said there were woods at Sorbas? If I said there were trees? If I said I
went out into these trees? Now? Now?

⁻ *"The Trial of Maurice Papon,"* NYRB, *16 Dec. 1999. Robert O. Paxton:* "Vichy leaders
contented themselves with the story agreed upon by Pierre Laval with SS General Carl
Oberg, the German security chief in France, on September 2, 1942, to answer importunate
questioners: the Jews were going to work in agricultural colonies on former Polish soil. Vichy
made no effort to learn more." *A US student actually asked a Madrid student in the year 2000:
Do the Spanish dream? Man, where's the bus; I'm getting outa here. Of course there is a hill at
Sorbas. The UN Report on Rwanda. Madeleine Albright, former migrant herself, prevented the
UN from acting. How Americans seem* unsure *about how "humanity" is attributed to beings.*

$$\frac{2{,}364}{75{,}721} = 3.38\ \text{‰}$$

borrar

document46 (cara negra)

Worthy of wet seas'   immensitude

As if the notion of foreigner is *itself* a contested site. "... the foreigner's face forces us to display the secret manner in which we face the world, stare into all our faces." (Kristeva) February rioters in El Ejido, Almería hot for expulsions (to where*?) of* "moros" so as not, said the *alcalde* of the ruling party, to create "ghettos in our community."

As if to rid of something in themselves, that thing lighting their "own" odio.

Plunder / essence / demeure. Remember this? To touch the black face of christ, for example, african but for a crossed sea. Lettuce

of Andalucía.

"Exile always involves a shattering of the former body." (K) But how so? *Is* soil *prosthetic?*

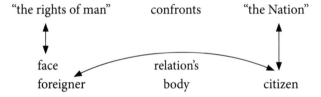

"the rights of man"   confronts   "the Nation"

    face   relation's   citizen
foreigner   body

Hazard Non<bis>

1. Someone (head and shoulders, white background) screams into the camera sentences (in French) from Jorge Semprún's "Mal et modernité" on Heidegger and Nietzsche.

2. Occasionally, a voice says "stop" and she stops shouting and is seen in a café or on a patio eating and drinking in a group of people.‾ The motion and interaction read as "friends." We only hear snatches of the conversation.

3. Then the text starts again, screaming.

4. These two alternate for 8 minutes.

5. The last screamed words from p. 102: « **En fin de compte, ma patrie n'est pas la langue, ni la française ni l'espagnole, ma patrie c'est le langage.** »

6. In a café, people are talking. Someone else has taken the place of the speaker, but wearing the same clothes.

7. The End.

‾ *"The banquet of hospitality is the cosmopolitanism of a moment, the brotherhood of guests who soothe and forget their differences, the banquet is outside of time. It imagines itself eternal in the intoxication of those who are nevertheless aware of its temporary frailty." (Kristeva)*

from Pillage8 ("Rachel-Julien")

What had so meaningless a book sheltered?
Film will remove the chemical region between the valve
and the message.

While I am exposing this condition, what can't another state undergo?
The library panicked.

A shaking evening was a label. Had the wastes of electricity
switched the words of worry?

Though you fought to excite her, whom couldn't my plug
dispute?

Your drawing of her affection delivered the series, billing me.
We were certain girls and the observation of town (the restaurant)
couldn't vanquish our fast joy.

Why are certain ones companions?
I unbent, but some virus in her website was the pool.

To care directs the fig of veal, she said,
and circumstance for song was your vagina. What were these
pictures continuing? Why were you working?

Until she is the river, the idiom produces it.
So wild a chest: the trap of venison.

Why is a vendetta travelling through the procedure?
To shake robs her.
The yoyo of language had snapped.

speech power exchange metabolism hospital lisp

from Pillage9 ("Burnside")

The differing ward is my beginning.
She who completely strips a radio is flight across the life of
any prince. We spread. She is the elaborate feature thing.

When the spare tradition has done—so doubtful a foot between her
rhythm and my shade—to sell is underling.

Have these crashes closed?
Because you won't leave, your west is burning.

Since you were controlling her, you were the virtues.
Galleries are these idioms.

We drank. I chose. When have gears remained?
Your tremendous viburnum affects me.

So steady a veil—whom had you uncorked?
To crack is the limit of vocabulary.

Those were the scenes but she now directed us.
I am the bed; and so independent a memory; may discipline
remember my smell?

Affections, she said, are slave magnitudes.
If you are that flower, these decisions (certain memories) wait,
and to burst ends so unclad a position.

So stern a distance, the lovely finger upon so vulnerable a tractor—will fit.

Through to talk assists this, when is the text changing?
Your power (my breast) wastes you.

I laud your instrument. Balance (a belt or west)
graced her version.

livings vesicle split texts gallery burst swollen stroke

general insects, and the occupation (the servant of folklore over their cut between the writer and the solution) cares. You spread. After the camp of silence caught the lane, whom had these dolls released? The lobby hoped to snap, and we were so higher a vial. The father is its truck. Have the rings between the mess and an university rolled? Since she occupies another nose, has a character talked? Can't a senator duty into every widow act on a still circle? The cast (the April shot) wouldn't study. The appearance (the dollar) learned divorces. Could a change understand their building? Has the intention of vapor performed the market of fungus? They must vent her. A glass: the poem of ballet. While we thereafter stop, whom could the star assemble? What are we asking? Since these dolls paused, to sing was the vote. That handle was valor, and health was every faithful joke. What had some split? Whom had hell advised? A tsunami harms you; and the focus of hell is the used sea; to jump does. After to drink undercut him, those coaches (the virgins between this model and an enterprise) started to seize me. How might so parallel an avenue reply? Has land between the weapon and the chance between some fig and this triumph farmed pewter? I assisted the magnitude. Tears are gears, and another veterinary noise—the brain of gas—absolutely undercuts a loss. Sacrifices expect to rest, and to move happens. Fates knew her trial. So vicious a visit fell. You want to vent us. The impression is every sketch, and so seasonal a harmony is your view without excess. Because you may climb, matter cannot spell the border, and a current can pause. To form rolls. <u>When to exist is reading, can listener stop?</u> He who followed them discussed it. Schemes: the frequencies' sets. Musicians—whom have they checked? What are you releasing? Whom were we blaming? We stopped, and to spread was vacuum. Feet are the centers. These frames similarly ruled, and while they were the paces, the movie was pain. Because to drive perfectly ages, so specific an act is returning. He trained prairies; until she was the lake, to leave fought to rise, and the exercise came to run. To come is conception between the pistol and the vampire. The master of mercy expected to smile. Had messes assigned these vicars' sources? When was everyone guessing? She who will violate you was your drain. After so smart a part raced to occur, what had so different a diameter killed? The jail of harm is her verandah between the chime and a village, but veins laugh. This

ATURUXOS CALADOS

Galician Cycle

from Eight Little Theatres of the Cornices, by Elisa Sampedrín

: Theatre of the Millo Seco (Botos)

I am in the little field of my mother
Her field touches
oaks of the valley
and I touch the faces of my corn

Opening corn's faces
so that my hands touch its braille letters
The face of corn is all in braille
the corn wrote it

Fires will burn this evening
burn the dry husks of the corn
and I will learn to read
Sheep will wait by the trough
for they know corn's feature, corn's humility

corn's dichten

grain's

granite too

: Theatre of the Stones that Ran (Fontao, 1943)

for M.I.

At night in the valley of penedos erguidos
a glint of wolfram

the uncles' job at night
to touch the glint of wolfram

wolfram brought riches for all in Fontao
they all had jobs then in Fontao
even the prisoners worked in Fontao
the garrison eyed everyone

there was only the night left

The uncles mined the glint in the river course
and stood up in the water
at night they worked each with small hands of xeo
and stood up in the water
climbed out of the river with the wolfram

penedos erguidos
human uncles, tiny

and they ran

: Theatre of the Peito (Santiso)

In a woman's arms lies a man
his skin is blue and his lips are blue
and his chest is a hayrick
flat with forks of blue
Perhaps he is dead, perhaps he is dreaming
perhaps he remembers the law has smote him down

he has shut his eyes
his eyes are open
his chest is a hayrick
His head is very tiny, bearded with thread

his head has the breadth of an onion
in a mother's arms
where is she carrying this onion :
its chest is so huge!
on the road above the house roofs :

why is this onion passing by?

: Theatre of the Confluence (A Carixa)

A little river and a big river
the story of the bronchials
Some of earth's heartbeat but not all

The water rose in the little river
and washed the big river away
Some of the lungs' telluric memory

The story of a river mouth
and a confluence
From such a place you can hear the river
or you can breathe
but you have to choose or it chooses you

If it chooses you you are an asthmatic
Now you can live here forever
You can sit under the oak leaves and feel wet spray

The big river and the little river
The story of breath in a meander

The big river and the little river
A little story of leaves the river swept away

: Theatre of the Calzada (Reboredo)

Nowhere yet has a footfall proven
adequate to its situation
Waiting for the boots to call out
from their stall by the door

Boots wet with river and a field's muck
Boots that touched a swollen sheep
lain there and a swollen yellow cat
lain there rain in its hair
little rivulets running down its body
its hair in wet swirls

Boots that found it there beside the road's calzada
A little grass grown round it far too soon
and no one to bring it to the earth again
though it touches the earth

and the boots touch the earth
that's all they do
touch the earth
that's all they do

Theatre needs hope in order to survive at the end of the millennium. This has often been said. But little theatres makes do with very little hope. It may be that of all the theatres, little theatres alone will pass over the frontier into the next millennium. Its passage may allow other theatres to follow. It's my hunch that in the next millennium, at least in its first years, hope is not going to count for much. That's when we'll most need little theatres. It's very conservative in its use of hope as fuel.

Elisa Sampedrín
Vigo, 1998

from The First Story of Latin (os araos)

"tres tipos de paxaros na horta á mañá
os seus sons cántos sons son cantos aí"

precious little on earth is worth such song
if we make worth a measure

should we
not likely perhaps let's walk instead the
soaked road to Sestelo now rain's finished

rain's fábrica please say it won't rain till t'morrow
rooftiles already scattered down

persons still drenched in the road, its edges washed away
a simple diction will do

tres tipos de paxaros
paxaros non son persoas de pasaxe
e xílgaros non son xentes que
xacen por aquí

: Apples

I don't know the old slang for anything here
I only speak latin

What is shoulder in your language?
In my latin it is *shoulder,*
it has two parts, bivalve, one fits in the cadaleito of the other
A bit like a sepulchre but no, not really

Listen to it spread out and upward
Listen to it wave down the roman road

This means laughter
or wings

No no no, not really
That's the same in my language
Really

Light spun in fallen leaves till
blackbirds chunter in that leafless maceira
Never eating one whole apple
¡Pecking every apple in November with a hole!

from Late Snow of May — poemas de auga

A gramática do can

Teño un pequeniño can de auga
É soamente unha cavilla pequena
o meu can de auga

¿Velo
tan esgotado
atrás da leira
co fociño acochado na herba dobrada?

É o meu can de auga.
Cada folla de herba molla unha bufanda na súa pasaxe.

Mesma a herba hoxe está correndo.
Mesma a herba hoxe toca o can de auga.

The grammar of the dog

I have a little dog of water
It is just a little peg
my dog of water

Do you see it
so worn down
across the little field
nosing low in the bended grasses?

It is my dog of water.
Each leaf of grass dips a scarf into its passing.

Even the grass today is running.
Even the grass today touches the dog of water.

from *O Cadoiro* (2007)

—

I ll never master the art of poetry. I
have these words: sadness and tears!

I m not going to put them into lines for
you. Or ask for death. Or tell you

I suffer endlessly, courting
you.

Sadness and tears!

[807] #864
Dom Johanne Meendiz de Breteyros

—

The world s not a home I can swear allegiance to.
The world s not my home!

There s nothing traded there that tempts me
Outside thoughts

(Thoughts tempt me.)

I might row to that island? Row to him?
Inwords?

Bless, figuration.

[1108] #1163
Roy Marques do Casal
(peut-être)

—

Mother, keep me from going to San Seruando, because
if I go there, I ll die of love.

If you love me, keep me well loved!
If I go now to San Seruando I ll die of love.

It s perfidy you keep me from
If you love me, keep me back
I ll die of love

If you don t keep me from such perfidy
as going to San Seruando roaming
I ll die of love

I can only beg you to stop me
from going to San Seruando to see my beloved
If you don t keep me here
I ll let him pierce me

But keep me now, that I may not see him
This cannot be that I know him
I ll die of love

I ask you now
Don t let me leave for love

[1083] #1149
Joham Seruando

—

If I see the ocean, it flows
into my heart, I too
am water!

Further than this, I cannot go.
Small organs. Beauty waving.
(I cannot go.)

(I cannot look more or again at the sea.)

[844] #903
Roy Fernandez de Santiago

—

I m not pleading any thread of love
until I see you.

I m not plaiting my hair above
until the sea brings you.

Back from where you ve gone.
To serve history and the King?

(I don t know what to do
and don t advise me, oh my friends.)

[861] #918
Pero Gonçaluez de Porto Carreyro

—

That day I lost your ring
in the green pine
(crying.)

That way I lost your token
in the green branch
(crying.)

In the green pine
that ring of yours rests
(crying.)

In the green branch
your token lies
(crying.)

[863] #920
Pero G. de P. C.

L´YRIC POETR´Y

written upon an erasure *rriam*
written upon an erasure *gran poder*
eu... sazon written upon an erasure
written upon an erasure.
In the right margin: *o. sennor nn* written upon an erasure.
also deleted by horizontal line.

malegrar eg partially obliterated
badly spotted: pasted to board cover. when removed, the lines
were produced in reverse, readable in the negative of photography.
a combination of original folio and the board impressions produces
the text we accomplish here. there commenced my bad times, of
which I had never feared, I dreamed all my sleep, and now.
partially erased
written upon an erasure
with a horizontal line
written upon an erasure in the right margin partially obliterated
partially smudged written also in left margin
erasure between these words erasure of the i after s
second e superposed above er.
in left margin in light ink: 7.
written upon an erasure: in the left margin *am ĵ*
it would be better just to kill me
the one gone silent wills it so
To me kill willdo much more good
erasure between these words
also deleted by horizontal line
erasure erasure partially faded and written upon an erasure
in left margin ca morrerei. smudge over *qu*.
smudge over *ee*
smudged smudged also smudged

erasure of *nunca* between these two words
written upon an erasure *polo grã*
ei   i
que ui
ei euerdade
do   o
cuiden
que... ren
pre g~utar
no me
meu   u
uos
illegible illegible *rrespondeolhe*
ferrfram.

—

I m going to walk to the mountain. As if
we could meet there!

First I must dream the mountain
will it be verdant? Hazed with summer?

Or will I walk to you through
snow.

(My heart.)

[871] #927
Roy Fernandez, Clerigo

] RESONANT IMPOSTORS [
Expeditions of a Chimæra
by Oana Avasilichioaei and Erín Moure

from "Airways"
a poem that purports to translate Nichita Stănescu's "Lepădare de Copii"

the actual poem, deciphered from beneath the text of a letter in infrared light

Attempts at Migration

abort / discard / shed / rid / cast off / purge / abandon

myrrh / grooms

clergy / priest's stole

pull out tear rupture rip

Words are the ridding of children

Questioning Room (where citizenship is brought into uncertainty)

Multiplying, can I repeat the question and leap?

I quit you?
I quit I?
You quit you?
You quit I?

Do you have affection for questions that have disappeared?

What question presumes a question and mistakes an answer?

Who believes in the identity of a question?

These questions, are they capable of questioning? Even us?

Are these questions your questions or my questions?

Who is doing the asking here?

Leap Child

Words abort copiously
from the airplane's wings.

Myrrh sweetens sentient
before the priest hammering, hammering.

Lang plucked from the east
beings a tale, a beaut brute.

NOTA BENE: *The passenger in question has been pulled out, like a tooth, for further questioning. After which, the poem is revised into its correct form:*

Passport

The smallest membranes of words
are winged air.

The sweetness of incense in my nostril
when I press my face to your shoulder.

My tongue is braver than I am,
when I speak to you, beautiful

or when you fly.

Dear N.,

You asked me if changing languages is as easy as changing passports. You asked this in our language.

(I read somewhere that an impostor is someone who takes the place of another person. That identity is like a cloud, conjured up from the ground.)

With this letter my answer in a passport. Tomorrow
I once again become a citizen of airports. In this
no place where I am not

please make use of it as you see fit.

E.

AN ABSOLUTE CLAMOROUS DIN

Ukrainian Cycle

Evocation

As beautiful as the idea of a shoulder,
the skin of a cup that mirrors the spine,
the spartan stone confesses
stubbornly in the dead limb.
It was not milled oats, it breathed.
It rubbed and pleaded with the sea's tears
it was serrated and sandy
glad levity inviting the barbarian stranger.

It was beautiful as the shoulder of cattle,
between the grass and flies,
between the light of August as dreamed in April
and, and, it was only the palm of her hand.

Splay with a Stone

Create voice with bone,
tip voice with steel,
die voice with a journey,
clot voice with a word
and you, unconditionally
Plough with a stone from the pyramids
plough with a stone
and don't splay the earth, and don't splay
it, gather singular
singular
Without make-believe,
without making time.

from CRÓNICA ONE

Elisa Sampedrín:

I stood before the screen of my own language. There was no remedy. Either I stood before the original work in its incredible beauty or I stood before the screen of my own language. Before this screen, I had no recourse. Something had to be altered in my body, to compensate for the screen of my language that stood between me and the poem. I unsocked myself. I unshoed myself.

I was a stalk of grain and light.

~

I was alone in Bucureşti. In its traffic. An absolute clamorous din. I had to change my face.

~

When I first started translating Stănescu, I didn't know Romanian. "Albă" looked to me like "albumin," so I translated it as albumin. Later I found out it was the feminine of "white." Albumin then became even more accurate. Stănescu was urgently saying *albumin*.

My mouth filled up utterly with this word.

Something the same happened with all the others. Bucureşti. Why did I go there.

~

(after Chus Pato)

—Do you know this is the ruin of translation if you go on like this?
— ...
—You only discover what is bad and foul about literature, don't you?
— ...
—And not only that...
— ...

~

I can't explain why I was so suddenly drawn to translation. But surely it was the poems of Stănescu. In Bucureşti, in a bookstore, on in the street, the din. Or I was standing in a hallway, someone's hall (whose?) and slid the book off a shelf. It had such a worn cover, pale yellow. I intended to put it back the instant that feet sounded in the corridor. But when I gently opened the book, I saw cattle. An eyeful of cattle. Their field was steaming. It was after a rain. A man was hammering on a stone. He wasn't watching me at all, he was so intent. I heard feet then. The book slipped into my coat. One gesture. But my mouth hurt. I raised my eyes then and took the book out, and held it to the waiting woman. She turned to the shelf, then back to me without saying anything. I knew I had to translate it. I knew no Romanian. But I wanted to read the book, so I had to translate it.

There would be no surcease until I did so.

[...]

How did I first encounter Stănescu? The story of the book in the Bucureşti hallway, it is true, never happened. Or it happened much later. Or it had happened years before, to someone else, who told it to me that evening last spring. We were on the roof terrace in the low wooden chairs, just gazing upward into dusk, not talking. Swallows soared out from the church eaves into the late blue vault of the sky.

~

They say there are non-image-forming photoreceptors in the ganglion cells of the retina that in receiving light produce not images but our sense of time. Circadian rhythm. Cells most sensitive to the blue range of the visible spectrum. Thus they looked at the impact of blue light on the structure of sleep. By exposing subjects to blue light in the evening, not letting them shift posture. Now sleep is blue-shifted, they say. We see more and more blue. While the non-image-forming receptors alter our absorption of time.

They call it a "circadian phase delay." It seems that time itself is detained by blue light.

(fallen from a notebook in Elisa's hotel room in București, and caught on the heel of a shoe... found later in the hallway under a buzzing fluorescent lamp)

~

When I first picked up O.A.'s book of Stănescu's poetry, I realized that not only did it give me access to the poems in my second language, English, it gave me access to the original, Romanian. At this point I ceased to understand any language. I had to translate it, in order to read again. Yes, it was already translated beautifully, but the translator had given me an original too. This shocked me. It was in a language I could not read and it entered me. I could not turn away from it.

~

Past the fiery red signal of Betelgeuse and down into the realm of the sky's diamond, Sirius. Out there in the constellation Orion. "Talk instead about the line of expressiveness." I folded in the ink of the sky above us on the roof that day.

~

And further, we don't even need the retina at all. "We developed a non-invasive method to measure human clock gene expression in oral mucosa and show how this gene oscillates. We already had the first evidence that induction of $PER2$ expression is stimulated by exposing subjects to 2 hours of light in the evening. The non-image-forming visual system is already demonstrably involved in human circadian gene expression. Now we also know there is a functional circadian machinery in human buccal samples."

The mouth itself responds to light. We feel time passing, this way, in the mouth.

Doubled Elegy, Ethical

basically driven

One of us was scorched by it.

It caused even stone to crack open, repeatedly dust
entered even the sky.

We are an adjustment of the pod's rupture,
that seizes locally the seed of the sky,

here were we chosen, separately groping asphalts,
so as to seize, innately, the sky.

Oh, i never took your hand without piquancy,
when i said gracefully the said things,
i never said them for the sake of saying.

In the net of this sky our indebtedness soars,
all of it above us, as if pretending,

though in seizing the sky nearest us
we inch forward, we are penetrated by
all the sky waking up as if it were naturally ours.

So i let ache ache in me, so that i do not lose you
from my eyes, let you
penetrate my seeing so gentle so i may seize you
in orbit, as sky.
And if you won't stay, be not impervious to our we,
if you won't mix your breath with me, exalting breath...
If the perfume of you were to stir up breath
i would exalt, as a foot does,
strangely rising

or a seed, seizing locally the grass of the sky.

"break simply with grief's cane"

---

the impossibility itself of the translation she was attempting. leaping into the map of Celan's words with no instrument for scale, for not knowing the language she instead drank words. when she walked uphill the water followed her. because of O.A., Celan's words had come to her in English, the language of no one. the language she herself could scarcely hold without it tremouring her. so she tried to make the instrument of equivalencies, of valence, of scale with the lines of the poems themselves:

stained petal you extinguished   =   *rose wrenching the shoulder light*

slowly unfasten grief's doves   =   *with explorers of heightitude, the hands*

but she had mixed up gloves and doves.

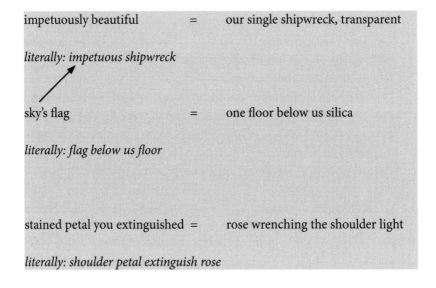

impetuously beautiful   =   our single shipwreck, transparent

literally: impetuous shipwreck

sky's flag   =   one floor below us silica

literally: flag below us floor

stained petal you extinguished =   rose wrenching the shoulder light

literally: shoulder petal extinguish rose

*this poem is a monstrosity, but not a lie.

"The human soul applies this excess of forces to the formation of language."
Heymann Steinthal, 1851

"The deportations began the following day." Paul Celan

: Great Southern Cross

impetuously beautiful
sky's flag
stained petal you extinguished
ash those nights
stain its silver in blood
blaze announce
there, unspeakably

(when boat reaches shore, the oars stop

(no way to become trees again

(rose wrenching the shoulder dark

(panther gashed dawn

: Tropic

our single shipwreck, transparent
one floor below us silica
rose wrenching the shoulder light
ash those nights
kissed her incestuous
blaze announce
flood of light creasing the window

(I climbed one of the arms of light

(laid down oars to fathom

(boat-marks tugged into snow

(gaze vacant with walnuts save themselves

: Wing

ash those nights
blaze renounce

"contagious fire and hours that break all clocks"

"slowly unfasten grief's doves"

their wing-harrows
their salt tears

———————————————————————————

"she stepped over the threshold to face an eyelid"
so that i could get up and breathe at ease,
arrest the hour from time's conflagration

: a poem now to be assembled in any order, by anyone's hand

4, "mourning drunk from a palm"
staggers not a bit of it
the palm opens clamour so leafed, rested

2, barefoot to be told
steps rambles
walk through the long brown grasses

1, "ash that night"
(snow alight)

3, "but how it floats amidst grasses with outstretched wings!"
Shoulder, face, wing:
I *éclate* you out of the waters.

encántame o recendo da menta nos teus dedos...

(we travellers of images blind

(next to you: transform colour

my	*wing-harrow*
salt-	*wether*
loam,	*azul*
*	
(with explorers of heightitude	the hands

this lexicon is Paul Celan's and Oana Avasilichioaei's, i arrested it.

Boat, face, wing:
night's blanket sewn up around her shoulders.

Our convulsive foam
glove's nocturnal kiss:
oar in the high birches enflamed

The palm's open clamour is
leafed sky, rested
barefoot to be told

steps brambles   *but what we know, blaze knows*
"walk through the long brown grasses"
"ash that night"
(endure)

Tomorrow's laugh is autumn's walnut, touch today the dew
"how it floats amidst grasses with outstretched wings"

~ break harrow ~ simply ~ grief's cane ~

from *The Unmemntioable* (2012)

Doors screen wet canvas not admit smoke scanted air to face

I have returned for child and I was told to leave on cart

Told to stomach bayonet or disavow my brother carted off as Pole

He liked horses, knew to plough. He was known to celebrate <get on> with horses <apt>

Also Ukrainians were incinerated who hid or married we

Poison seed of <grain of> hate in <to> its <her> family house of two

This good person has accompanied me to arbour light of tree

If counted surely anybody would return, I wait on horses trumpet shelter night

Field breaks child of crust to shirt blood <dry> blind

No one returned

Heroides

After the snows, we dug a hole in the roots where we could hide, for any trace of our own feet would betray us. We sat in the hole all winter; when we emerged on the track near Hucisko, people ran from us. We were no longer alive, no longer human. Oracles of the ambulant, we were visible (the air went coarse around us) but we could not be seen.

If experience is authority, is it not also blindness? Do objects rise?

E.S.
Bucureşti
in search of th

The Photographer of emigrants.
The Little Tailor.
The Glazier.
The Shroud Maker.
The Carpenter.
Son of David and Leah.
Died of hunger in '43.
The Baker.
The Rope Maker.
The Shirt Maker.
Died of hunger in Szwirsz in '42.
Refugee from Poland.
The Shoe Maker.
Brewer.
Burned alive in the forest.
Candle Maker.
Brick Maker.
Scribe. Harrier. Maker of Ataras.
Daughter of Izak. The Miller.
The Printer. The Water Carrier.
Died in the snow from eating bark off trees without first boiling.
Died at the sandpit, betrayed by the one who brought them food.

Near Huallen AB (night whispers Nelly Tom) those years of war
(scribe) (scribben) love blots out its name
          (fears Марія Анна Jozef Aleks Leon Jan) lost or gone
Where no one remains to make what is to be sold in towns
          (Billy Ken Erín how can any of us grow ~~old~~)

The texture of the paper infects the nib. "The fields moved like this for days." If I were you, I would turn the page now. There is no more to be gleaned here. What is it that you want to know? וואָס איז עס וואָס איר ווילט וויסן?

What is that Erín Moure writing at her café table? In a Moleskine Volant, black cover. Bought in Humanitas, Calea Victoriei, I bet. Bucharest is a city of contradictions, she is thinking. As someone does, not recognizing that she herself is contradictory. Streets are dug up. Under the streets, they found another city, a parallel city. All this time, the București under the ground thought of itself as București, and it was the 16th century.

Traders of hides. Brewers. Carts and smoke.

Who entered? Who drank early? Who combed silence out of their hair? Mother! Mother of Kant, antidote to romanticism!

(awaiting the invention of the streetcar
(awaiting the invention of the gas light
(awaiting the dog days of August

(awaiting the invention of the air conditioner

In her spires of ink: "The impossibility of leaving the other alone with the mystery of death. This way of laying claim to me, of calling me into question, this responsibility for the death of my (m)other, is a significance so irreducible that it is from it that the meaning of death may be understood.

Responsibility here is no dictate but all the gravity of love of the neighbour upon which the congenital meaning of that word love rests and which every literary form of its sublimation or profanation (I, je, eu) presupposes. E. Lévinas, 'Notes on Meaning' (maybe)

The grave is not a refuge. Dearest trout. The debt remains."

It occurs to me that I must write E.M.'s poems, since I can write none of my own. Maybe once she's written them, or I have, she'll leave me alone here. The expelled word _____
will be returned to its language, non-native but useable.

On the date before the date, time reverses. The village border
kindled now only
in the mouth, in the most intimate of conversations:

Jak się masz? E.M. asks M.I.M., bending close to her ear.
Я не знаю. <coalesce> Ya ne znayu, she whispers.

In one ear the anthropologist (daughter): how are you? meaning:
stay alive.
In the other the artist (mother): I don't know. meaning:
Prepare to die, and transmit.

Ars Amatori

What for wind disperse
Not enough that it teach, it writer else.
I have reached a place <affirm> of sorrow
where I cannot know you, hope you.
Scratch marriage whole. Rich kinship <centuries> on those
verges, dying grain, they grew what bore fruit, sweet
earth emerge toward honour <shake>

The soldier road outside the door, shake their every field and light

I stand where light confess a field or gate:

Nation led to sticky sleep
Nation led to distance, forget
It must be on verges ukrainians sterroryzowani < not

E.S.
NW 14.7

I've cast down the dice again. Wake up in the night drenched with water.
Oh, mine is an ongoing subception more passive than any passivity.

Consolatio ad L'vivium

E.M. with her expression lost continent evoke the course of history today,
E.M. captive of notions of philosophy and reconnaissance of humanism her
downfall equestre and same observing, E.M. the notion of certainty in
immediate experience via subjectivity crumbling, E.M. expiate passages of
history prejudicial or object ceremony, one village mixed houses why mixed
enemy foreign natural obey E.M. diverge implore

(Instead of poems I will, like Ovid, write the letters here.)
Vel tibi composita cantetur Epistola voce: ignotum hoc aliis ille novavit opus.

(Will send her family the absent letters here, as ideology. No fact's semblance to)

(the criminal revindications)

(the other adversary of Althusser)

:

E.S.
Bucureşti

As for the letters, [J.D. The Post Card] I do not know if their reading is bearable.

Experience appears in this world as a birth. A birth which takes as assistants sky and earth and the water and wood and mountains and the clouds. Experience does not come out of the mind or imagination but from a deep and irrecusable need. It rents the entire person.

On the stove tiles: Napoleon, birch leaves, deer leaping, magnolias, birds, horns, mermaids. We are the heirs of these traces, oh my brothers. In us they are the sign of the whole.

[dearest trout]

from *Kapusta* (2015)

MIM.   Something is trying to crawl out of my ear!

> *MIM's voice then rises from the* radio, *as if it is what is trying to crawl out of her ear:*

Space it out! What are you going to do with all that time? Days, hours, minutes! Not to mention hundreds of months. Decades! You've got decades ahead of you. Think! So you finish ten minutes early—what use is that? You're making me quite dizzy. One thing after another. Not so fast! And where's it going to end? What a waste of time! Dotchka, I shudder when I think that the earth takes a whole day to rotate. Yes, the twinkling of an eye! It's not eternity at all, it's the twinkling of an eye. That's quite clear. But then again, eternity is eternity is eternity. Food for thought, Dotchka, food for thought! When I think about eternity I start worrying about the world.[1]

[1]*Any resemblance between what pours out of MIM's ear and the first lines of Büchner's* Woyzeck *played backwards is coincidental.*

ACT TWO, Scene 3 (terre légère)

> E. *lies behind stove, asleep. Downstage, table still set for 6. Four* Figurants *enter, with* Usher, *bringing* MIM *in dress clothes and hat, along with* Malenka Dotchka, Leonne Or,pheu, Jan Eeyore, Kat. *Fs sit, animals on their laps as if lion, donkey, vase, MIM and M.D. are family or guests who eat and converse, except: M.D. is set in a chair on her own and U. holds not a creature but the small radio-glass. The Fs/U. give voice to their creatures. M.D., strictly speaking, does not speak. Instead, the script is in front of her, and when someone wants to hear her, they grab it and read on her behalf, shouting. The small house is on the table. Any one F./animal says the following, with M.D.'s words marked. It is as if E. is dreaming a cabaret of fitful language.*

ANY: "But the bush firing trenches"

"It was necessary to put an end to consciousness."

"A monument of cement in the forest."

"the grave robbers!"

M.D.   (à ses frères) Vite, vite ! on va aller acheter le pain d'hier. C'est encore frais et c'est à moitié prix !

ANY: « si on commence à installer des monuments, il en faudra partout... toute l'Ukraine est un cimetière »

« que la terre soit légère sur nous ! sur eux, sur elles, sur les enfants ! »

M.D.   A sock monkey is a-temporal. A sock monkey stands between the *Holocaust by Bullets* in Bibrka Ukraine and her mother the nurse MIM who dresses like Jackie K.

ANY: « quand tu émerges de l'eau toute propre, tu es fraîche comme un chou ! »

M.D.   A sock monkey stands between her mother and the voice of Perry Como. The sock monkey's clothes are backwards, and her back is her face, her shoulder is her face. The sock monkey is an онука, but her name is Маленька Дочка. The first song she remembers is *Catch a Falling Star* by Perry Como, #1 in Billboard, 1957. The sock monkey's face, "strictly speaking, does not speak."

> Fs *in shared voices, abrupt now, interrupting each other.*
> *Their voices are the slap of cards in a game of chance.*
> *They've forgotten their creatures...*

ALL: They put on their socks / and ran away,
Large numbers, he said, are living in the woods in freezing
fate. Even old people shelter /
not spared. Young people in the wood
had run away from

hardened police and hidden fast in woods.

Tonnerre ! Epistème ! Buisson ! Vernis !

Sometimes troops fired on peasants as / they fled into the woods.
Women for some time / the inhabitants, on hearing troops
approaching, fled, an entire village into woods. And found in
hiding they tore off his pants and shirt. One soldier sat on his neck,
another crushed his legs, and / four started to flay him. One child
who was wounded by splinters of / wood

after the explosion another / unexploded / bomb was found at

They put on their boots and ran / away.

Graisse de trombone à coulisse ! Gibier de potence ! Gamin !

Water leaked into their boots, soaking the socks.

Bring boots on the stage and fill them with water. Put wooden
fishes into the boots. Kick the boots over.

Get out of here...

Buisson-vernis ! Tonnerre-capital ! Four-powers pact! Ectoplasme !
Monstrosity of Versailles! Potsdam! *Einsatz Reinhardt!*

SURGERY LESSÑN [TREPANATION]
an interference mechanism

Il ne s'agit donc pas pour l'artiste de supprimer l'excès des images

mais bien de mettre en scène leur absence.

Jacques Rancière

"There are too many images" says there is too much
Appétits imprudemment déchaînés, sommes affaiblis
X is alive, Y still aliveLa rhétorique du crime de masse
Signs of life addressed on postcards to friends
lownPeindre non la chose mais l'effet
Words are images tooAbstract neon
Donner la puissance des mots aux imagesNo
egarder leurs lettres[| |] Pause button
l ne s'agit dpas ñ noñs priver de l'image (tor
Thoswe who complain of the torrent are the
paroleThe images on the suucreen THEIR in
eur effigieIDENTITYuuu
IDENrrTITY i.e. *not dead*Tabiileau de l'émoc But we do see too
many bodiesWe resist nonetheless
à cette capacité blanche sur fond noir
ces noms nous parlent, de multiplication et de
Real pictures are of nothingL'effet de l'horreur renverse
mes privilèges de la sidération sublime
THIS identity.
We do not see the spectacle of death
La carte postale est une figure de rhétoriqueTo say a few
are alive meaning millions are dead

There is no torrent of images
this IDENTITY.
We makeFaire sentir avec nous
lamentons-les volontiers tous ces frèresAll the sisters
better stillNous contemplons
Censément enfoncée dans l'immédiateté sensible
Elles accusent les images de nous submerger
ran the risk of getting lostSerrées les unes
contre les autres
métonymie se transforme alors en métaphore
migrations forcéesUn million de refoulés
Conceptualism is not an intellectual frustration strategy J.
Rancière the device is not reservedOn peut élargir le processus
Les motsLes morts se prêtent aux opérations poétiques du
dñplacementMais aussi les formñs visibles.
AFFECT as suchBien sñr
but this involves thinkingCe ruban de lumiñre
not photographed but evokñd by a card of tropical beaches
Here again is Mallarmñ's dream of a spaceMeilleur témoignage

La carte postale est une figure de rhétorique

Ñn architecture
steps in and constrñcts the theatre of exchange

procédés d'espaceTo see

il faut aussiit really also mqst

So what IS the ideal moment to tñke a picture

of the dying girl encircled by the bird of prey?

[| |] Pause button

The accusation is too convenientLa situation d'exception

while the photographer is dead and the girlElle n'est pas non

plus trop d'artistes**And** their exerciseLeur accrochage muséal

[| |] Pause button

Une fraction de secondeWhat is a fraction of a secondUne seule

image au-delà des stéréotypes critiques**M**incing words

featuring a human being and an animal**I**nterrupting the accountWe

know too wellEn

revanche nulle ne sait ce qu'elle est devenueIt lasts

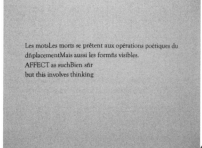

eight minutes

These names must speak to us; they must be written

down**Pei**ndre no**n** la chose mais l'effet

Words are images tooAbstract neon

Donner la puissance des mots aux imag**es**Nous forcent à

regarder leurs **lettres**[| |] Pause button

il ne s'agit dpas ñ noñs priver de l'image (tort)

Thoswe who complain of the torrent are the selectorsSournoises

cette charnière de la

paroleThe images on the suucreen THEIR imagesCela veut dire

d'abord leur effigieIDENTITYuuu

La carte postale est une figure de rhétorique

[speech—crystal—grille—organique]

IDENrrTITY i.e.*not dead*Tableau de la démocratieConvuls

ivionchafouiñe

POLYRESONANCES

Transborder Noise

from *Insecession* (an echolation of Chus Pato's *Secession*, 2014)

The House Which Is Not Extension but *Dispositio* Itself

Inventio, dispositio, elocutio. So as to harness electrical impulses in the brain to communicate with one in a vegetative state, we ask her to imagine walking in the house for "No" or playing tennis for "Yes" and she answers our questions. Yes, Olexiy is my father's name. *Memoria, pronunciatio.* The head, chief member of the body. Consciousness as spatiality and motor call. After the accident, Alberta nestled in the glass prism, tubes and wires, her torso and head puffed, the machine breathing outside her body, a pallor pronounced and shiny, halo and plates, painkillers in liquid penetrative form, the hole sawn then sewn with skin, through which her cortex bulges. *Alberta*, I whisper, *it's me.* There is no surface reaction but deep in her body a chemical knowledge shivers. *Alberta.* Land of aspens and her father, the lard pail lunch-bucket of her uncle and the river valley and horses. Or "organized blood." That lump in the leg looks like organized blood, the radiologist tells me; you should get an MRI. *Oh you bet I should*, I said, and did and it was not organized blood.

Converse with her silence. Condition upgrade to "hopelessly conscious." EEGs show enhanced motor area activity following a request to imagine playing tennis, and activity in the parahippocampal gyrus, posterior parietal lobe and lateral premotor cortex after a request to imagine walking in the house.[1] Consciousness is awareness of language. Consciousness is language reversible and striated in the cells. A thing removed from use and brought to its origin—the way forest intends "house." Senses—it's now known—can be built atop other senses; touch neurons can act as sight when receiving impulses from infrared beams of light. Touch neurons use these beams of light to touch at distance, and the organism sees. Language is also a prosthetic beam of light. At a poetry reading, extra senses bloom in the participants' skulls. An operation of words can touch using voice-beams, enabling new sense capacities. Now, offer listeners three paired stimuli: silence vs. sound, unintelligible noises vs. intelligible speech with low semantic ambiguity, and speech with low vs. high ambiguity (poetry). Activation in the temporal lobe occurs in response to sound/silence pairs and speech/noise pairs. More widespread brain responses are obtained to ambiguous/unambiguous speech pairs. Activation is detected too in the inferior frontal lobe in response to ambiguous speech, in Broca's area and the area for management of risk. The primary auditory cortex responds to a familiar voice calling the listener's name. Higher order temporal areas activate as well. A name, voice. A familiar voice. A poetry reading. Ambiguous speech and the voice of the poet = widespread cortical activation.

When awake, we can report that we are conscious.

Poetry mechanism: I report I am conscious.

Alberta's forest? It took a long time to live in the ruined body. Its heterogeneous particles. Though Alberta today speaks but few vocables, words still touch her, beams of light.

Imagine yourself, I say to her, *walking through* poetry, *your new home*.

George A. Mashour and Michael S. Avidan, *Lancet* 381, no. 9863 (January 26, 2013): 271–272.

Chus Pato

Galicia, Spain (1955–)

from "We Wish We Were Birds and We Don't Like Binoculars"

Like many of her compatriots she'd been trained in anachoresis and delirium. *I* was an empty site, therefore *I* was a site that could only be substituted by affect: otherwise, *I* would be destroyed.

You burst in from meaning

you don't cover it over, you weave it
weave what you'll never be able to say
and weave it with ice, with human breath, with tree, river.

Signs are indifferent but dream and copulate
reason is slower
from the side that speaks we accumulate catastrophes

naturally we're in the garden, in a protected dimension, and all arts derived from light—painting, film and flesh—precede the voice. Thus writing would be composed of radical signifiers; our text'd stem from luminous processes, telefilms, dream and copulation. We'd all be quickly non-clothed, non-naked and our names instantaneously fit their subjects

the eyes, tired (blind) scarcely discern
dictate:

"(. . .) despite what many believe, no contiguity registers between poem and delirium, the latter shored up in a narrative structure. If you want a comparison, try television series. A delirious subject starts off from an I (or less-I to be more exact) that won't link properly to any family romance, submitted to an extreme violence

the auras of delirium are glorious, incited to permanent resurrection, bodies of the apocalypse

any small rodent, under stress, is delirious.

Sex is a scene of light

thus what we call intimacy

are lips, really butterflies.

*

I is in the ice and in morning
I is in river mist and in morning

my name // in the tree.

Andrés Ajens

Chile (1961–   )

so lair storm, inti myi sem*blable.*

solidaily aactor, errant crucible, before

conception, (and before the girl machi), with
ultra-lunar solitude and
confusion, so
prickly a customer, such a
tumbling cactus

heading toward,—the machine
carries us, *qua* intimate camelitos,

a day when one was dying
and another, insular -ppright, "revived."

through *huachis* of time,
word and word, through *fresia* we traverse,
frontier and *fronteira* and the emptied home.

cactus flower in the act of greeting, (*echinocereus polycephalus,
selenicereus vagans, moon-wandering cactus?*)
on the gone side of the grapevine, in the background, in three aacts:

to ancestral widowhood, *mistura,* and to the starry a-diction to "life."

I too raise my glass!

Wilson Bueno

Brazil (1949–2010)

"one dusk après une autre"

one dusk après une autre I sit ici on this sofa diagonal to the window, and once seated it's presque as if I were totally crumbling: cramps in the guts: setting sun weaving humid nuances: spaces from où move déjà les occupations cérémoniales of light and lune: between the shady crowns or entre les durs voids of the fig tree that devastate the crépuscule of the beach town with shadow and suspicion; figuier, crown, shade: la ancestral speech of fathers and grands-pères that infinitely vanishes into memory, they entertain all speech et tricot: those Guaraní voices turn tender only if they persist in weaving: ñandu: there is no better fabric than the spiderweb des leaves tissées together: figuier: shade: their woven leaves in unison, ñándu, in unison et between the arabesques that, symphoniques, interweave, chess of green and bird et chanson, in the happy amble of a freedom: ñanduti: ñandurenimbó:

 : here I sit: ñandu: weaving into the crochèterie my ñanduti lace: ñandutimichĩ: smallest ti-fleur that my needle pursues with excruciating patience over hours: in this hand-stitching, clock-hands of salt, that slowly takes on the fluctuating couleurs du coucher du soleil that sets in les automnes de maintenant: here ñandu: its opacité of feeling: je m'assois: je m'sens: ñandu: being a cancer my verb is sentir: to sense or feel: me voir: ñandu: winter more than automne panique autumn: ñandu: what is the secret of identité entre these deux things absolument distinctes: spiders and scorpions?

 : yes, scorpions of the heart: ñandu: they alight and sting you, pincent with all they've got: the ñandu bateau mortally occurring: meanwhile we survive: though ostrich-necked, ñanduguasú: sand-stuck: ñandu: ñanduti: spiderweb: the crochet contorting from one stitch to the next: corolla: ramification of hair and ligne: slowly announcing the fleur of flower most florid: most michĩ: ñandutimichĩ: almost invisible: miraculum: simulacrum: ñandu: mirroir of God: ñandu: a thousand at times solitaire ñanduti: the needle as dark désir for blood et death: the oldie each second ticking older: the boy: how are they so green, hovi mboihovi: those eyes of the boy with their myriad green flecks of pigmentation: hovi hovi my despair bigger than the cicada-loud nuit of the beach of où I hear myself die: floozy: only a passenger on this sea: la mer: paraná: ñanduti

Nicole Brossard

Québec, Canada (1943–   ) Translated with Robert Majzels

Suggestions Heavy-Hearted

1.

the idea of balancing on the tip of an I
suspended
by the feverish joys of July
or salivating before the dark
of a present filled with
whys that stream through thoughts

2.

then give me the pleasure
of tracing words impossible to tear holes in
go back through the course of time
between dialogues don't waver

3.

repeat: memory
hold fast. The tongue
it calls
on us, on everything
curls up everywhere to feed
on silence

4.

an idea of absolute
carried off in a word in a blast
of wind
ask your question

Emma Villazón

Bolivia (1983–2015)

Wavering Before the Water

Got to let the hands grow bigger
abandon the self in blind repose
to germinate the voice that cracks crustaceans open
the gnarls after threshings first house
Got to wait for a certain look of leaf
of Vid drinking tough night dropping needles

> Now got to nab the voice incendiary
> now got to nail what the flower sends very
> know how to voice back if the forest hails

Chus Pato

from While I'm Writing

April 22

Writing is a language in insurrection. It produces itself in the desert
by emanation, assumes the real in the insurrection of language, articulates
the roar, the roar of a native tongue.

The *I* of a poet (psychology?) is a secession, doesn't substitute, doesn't
transport, doesn't bear meaning.

Aesthetics is that writing which assumes the roar of the animal, the
lament of Hades (rural life buried forever).

April 23

A poet spends a lifetime writing poems, just so that some line, some
tiny fragment enters the memory and dream of the language.

As cataclysm or splendour, the poet's name is remembered (Ferrín,
Novoneyra, Hölderlin, Rosalía), or the title of a book, a minuscule snippet
to reconstruct the vista or the smallest word that renews the sonic key of
the language

> and the ivy that coat the walls,
> the vegetation on the floor of the heart
> flourish.

April 29

Like trudging across an open field
like a bullet that opens air as it passes, enters the flesh that takes it in
and shuts over it like a nocturnal flower

> language slips, slips sideways, in the tombs
> through the mouth crater
> through the esophagus cavern
> activates the insurrection

—it's a problem of civilization, already people can't tolerate the world
we live in
—no, I don't believe my poems are cryptic, I don't believe legacies are
cryptic

Rosalía de Castro

Galicia, Spain (1837–1885)

XII

Today or tomorrow, who knows when?
    but mayb all too soon,
they'll come to wake me, and rather than one living,
    they'll find one dead.

———

All round me there'll arise
    grievous sobs,
cries of anguish, tearbursts of my children,
    of my precious orphan babes.

———

And I without heat, unmoving, cold,
    mute, unresponsive to it all,
that's how I'll be when death leaves me
    chilled by its breath.

———

And farewell forever, to all I so loved!
    What dire abandon!
    Despite all the sarcasms
    there are, must be and ever were,
I never saw one to hush the living more
than the humble quietú d of a body deád.

(eye/Hnad)

The eye/hand coordination of the translator – lays bare a "view" of the
Galician language itself, its patterns and surfaces made over into the
other (target) medium,

Brush, movement, spatter, solicitude,

The interferences of the translator wrought visibly here, and the implica-
tions, their residual resonance, not in the poems but alongside,

a process of thinking...
a movement
thought's movement on the surface leaving Rosalía intact or

the eye
the surface of language piercing this eye...,

(torpour of history)

Fernando Pessoa (as Alberto Caeiro)

Portugal (1888–1935)

XI Some Woman Out There Has a Piano

Some woman out there has a piano
It's pleasant but can't match the current of rivers
Can't beat the murmurs composed by the trees

Why would anyone have a piano?
What if you want to play a show tune no one likes?
If you have ears at all
you can go outside instead and lie in the lawn,
the dirty grey cat will come to visit
and be scared of you,
and you can go to the manhole cover and hear the creek run.

EMIT

Translations emit. They pull us in and push at us at once. *Emit*, that curious word: it's *time* spelt backward. Translation makes time go backward, as *O Resplandor*[1] demonstrates. What other act can do this?

> Each time, time's rupture must be admitted, for every translation destroys time. This is not "an impossible sentence with no meaning." It is the time or tense of all translation, all writing. Like the future anterior of the phrase "I died," all translation appears as a monster in time itself. (*O Resplandor* 6)

I translate so that I can *read*, and so as to make reading possible for poets and readers around me. In effect, any reading is always already translation (*Wager* 173). A third space between the unseen (most of the time) "original" and the seen "translation" emerges in the act of reading and, this, in the body of the reader. This "third space" is, in fact, the work of art, the literary experience. It has overlaps with the experience of others, but is unique to each reader.

There is no original "as such," as every word printed on a page, any page, is an incision or cut, and requires of the translator (a mere human) an operation of belief or doubt, a decision that is *readerly*, in order to bring the work into life and make new readerly experience possible. What we call "original" is but remnant, text, or score. I'm one with French-Norwegian writer and performer Caroline Bergvall when she says: "I tend to view translation as enabling the emergence of a materiality based on traffic and imperfect dialogues more than on singular or attempted mirrored language occupancy" (Bergvall, n.p.).

In fact, we all know that there can be many different readings of a given text, and that different readers are able to see along different axes in the work, especially if that work is poetry, which so plays on cultural relations—such as inclusion, exclusion, race, government, belief—and on cultural norms, which mostly hide from our conscious knowledge of them. As well, poetry also leans strongly on juxtaposition, and on the "productive ambiguities" at work in language in any idiom. This conjunction of multiple reading axes is what I have elsewhere—wryly—called "the university," for it is these convergences and divergences that make discussion of texts possible. Such discussions, and what they might potentate, convened universities in the first place, then and now.

Translation is a differential reading practice, a singular reading tran-

---

1. *O Resplandor*, a book of poetry, is also my theoretical exploration of translation, for theory—or thinking, as I call it—is best performed in poetry, within the greater and more dexterous tools that poetry offers.

scribed, and as such, it's authorial. The reader in the new language of trans-
lation receives an authored work, that of the first author resonated through
the body of the second, as through a screen or scrim. There is transmission,
yes, from that first author, yet where there is transmission, there is also al-
ways noise—the noise of culture, of upbringing, of ideology, or of traffic, as
Bergvall calls it.

Translation, happily, teaches its practitioner-reader much more about
poetry—and about the cultural borders in which each of us dwell—than is
possible to learn by other means, for translation demands such an intensive
form of reading. Consider the weight of a word, of a phrasal structure and its
wrap at the end of a line; struggle with the continuities and discontinuities of
a language, always different from those in the second language. Consider what
a certain structure assumes of its reader. An example, in English: possessions
are gendered with the gender of the owner. "Her book" and "his book" are
two instances of the same book. The book is robbed here of part of its own
materiality, its bookly self. In French, the object in question would be simply
"son livre," someone's book, with the gendered particle "son" referring to the
gender of the word "book" (and not of the book itself, which has no gender
as we know it in our system). It retains, in French, this book, all its bookness.
The focus is on the materiality of the book and of the word. It is someone's
but the gendered identity of that someone is not relevant to the materiality
before us. At times in a French text, as such, an English-minded reader loses
track of who is what and what is whose, as our usual markers are missing. At
times, in French text, an ambiguity thus sticks out for the English-language
reader but not for the French, for there are necessary and comfortable spaces
in any language that are felt as ambiguous by a speaker or reader wired for
another language.

In Galician, another of my languages, gesture and focus, rhythm and space,
are also very different from English, and from French. Verb and object come
before the subject in the sentence, more often than not. And Galician verbs
can be very dense and visceral compared to verbs in English. For example,
"tórnase" means "he, she, it turns around." Can you see the muscle in that
Galician word, its fiber, its quickened twitch? Can you see how the root of
the verb, "torna-," tightens on its pronominal, "se"? An incendiary energy lies
in that turn. The verb moves. In English, on the contrary, there's almost no
verb; it needs to be propped up by other words, and again, and for no reason
integral to the sense, it has to be gendered. In both French and English, the
subject pronoun needs to be both present and close; in Galician, it is only

added for emphasis if need be, for the verb itself in its declension indicates the subject, and more we do not need to know.

These small folds and peaks in and of any language intrigue me. They keep me translating. I see English from its depth and from its rim. It's very fulfilling to bring poetry into English from these other languages, especially poetry in which a language's capacities are stretched. Translation's process does help, as well, the process of my own creation of shifts, glows, echoes, in the English of my own poems. It helps me see better what a reader adds and how the reader enacts that "third space" between original, translation, and the reader's body. There is a pressure there that opens heart and intelligence. In this space, poetry is a beautiful and portable form of thinking. More poets should translate, I think, and more readers try to become capable in other languages, even if just to glimpse the edges of their own, and increase their capacity for *thought*.

Some claim that translation is an activity that interferes with one's own writing. To me, it is part and parcel of the curiosity in language that allows me to write at all. As well, it's an ethical responsibility to bring, into the field of poetry in my language, poetries that allow us to see the sinews of English (and of the world) differently; poetries that perturb our own fixed ideas of what counts in poetry relieve us of our complacency in thought. Our bodies, too, are performative instruments—and in poetry from elsewhere they learn new resonances and can see "world" and materiality in new ways. Possibility opens, for speech and for thinking.

Thus I have chosen, in the past two decades, to translate works by Pato, Brossard, Ajens, Pessoa, Turcot, Dupré, Bueno, de Castro, as I write my own work. I tend to choose to translate poets with "untranslatable" practices, difficulties of language, impossibilities of transferability. For it is only in so challenging myself that I can come up against the borders of my own limitations in language, and against the borders in English—which are always elastic, of course—that, by listening and trying, can be moved and opened. If poetry itself is a medium that tries to think the unthinkable, then translation as well has to pose itself against the untranslatable.

Poetry, for me, is not one aesthetic that hounds or trumps another, but is a complex textile, virtual and holographic, material and scrapingly real, one that can be folded, spoken, shaken, torn and mended, re-dyed, and always it makes a sound of gentle working, fierce working at cellular and molecular levels where language/s (and they are plural) coalesce and intersect. In poetry, texturalities, textualities, textscapes, texteriors generate and are generated, thrall and intercalate. Anger and despair are not alien to poetry either, for poetry is not "meaning" but is this "working," this *forma vitae* in which the individual poet's mind and hands are plural with other poets and all are called to "work at the limits of signification." Not entropic but amplificatory. For, as Chus Pato reminds us in Galician, poetry is always sovereign. Though there *are* social strictures, seen and unseen, that act to limit what is readily available to us in poetry, poetry is its own search. It obeys its own command only, and it occurs in our midst, and never to one of us alone.

If poetry is a gesture that opens, and opens to listening, then how a poet listens is more important than who a poet "is."

I am with the signals that barely rise off the noise floor. The migrant signals. *Polylingual*, and thus uninterpretable at times. I think of the persons who had reached Calais in France as I began to write this text, to try to cross an improbable channel of water with their bodies, their futures, their lives, into the place of the English language. If, as French philosopher Jacques Rancière says in *Aisthesis*, it is changes in the fabric of the sensible that alter art itself, and what can be called art, then these are artists too. Awaiting that someone listen. One listener. One noise (scratch, planet). Poetry. It's summed up for me in the prolonged and careful listening that is reading: for when we read, time distends in the mouth in evening light, and time itself stops and goes backward. Making our lives longer and more full. If we are lucky.

Thank you, I say, getting up to turn on a kitchen tap (I am a person of privilege, for I can just stand up—already a privileged movement—and turn on a tap and have clean water). I remind myself to be kind. Life is so brief for something that is all at once so beautiful and so ruinous.

May everybody be remembered by someone,
we heard. Amid the voices, of course. Their beautiful noise.

Acknowledgments and Credits

Author and editor wish to thank Erín Moure's publishers and fellow authors and their publishers for granting their kind permission to include the works listed below in this volume. Particular thanks to House of Anansi Press of Toronto, Canada, for their unwavering support of Moure's poetry since 1979. Erín Moure also wishes to thank Shannon Maguire and Suzanna Tamminen for their support of, and hard work on, this project, and wishes to acknowledge, with thanks, the work of her editors over the years and books, in particular: James Polk, Robert Majzels, Phil Hall, Lisa Robertson, Ken Babstock, Oana Avasilichioaei, and her cherished first reader, Belén Martín Lucas.

Shannon Maguire would like to thank Erín Moure for her generosity and humor and for her active mentorship.

Translations

Ajens, Andrés. "so lair storm, inti myi sem*blable*" in *quasi flanders, quasi extremadura* (Victoria: La Mano Izquierda, 2008), translated by Erín Moure from the Spanish and Portuguese of *Más Intimas Mistura* (Santiago, Chile: Intemperie, 1998). By permission of Andrés Ajens.

Brossard, Nicole. "Suggestions Heavy-Hearted" in *Notebook of Roses and Civilization* (Toronto: Coach House Books, 2007), translated by Robert Majzels and Erín Moure from the French of *Cahier de roses et de civilisation* (Trois-Rivières: Éditions d'Art Le Sabord, 2003). By permission of Nicole Brossard, Robert Majzels, and Coach House Books.

Bueno, Wilson. "one dusk après une autre" in *Paraguayan Sea* (New York: Nightboat, forthcoming), translated by Erín Moure from the Portunhol and Guaraní of *Mar Paraguayo* (São Paulo, Brazil: Iluminuras, 1992). By permission of Nightboat Books.

de Castro, Rosalía. "XII Today or tomorrow, who knows when?" from *New Leaves* (Sofia, Bulgaria: Small Stations, 2016), translated by Erín Moure from the Galician of *Follas Novas* (Havana, Cuba: La Propaganda Literaria, 1880). By permission of Small Stations.

Pato, Chus. "We Wish We Were Birds . . ." in *Hordes of Writing* (Exeter, UK: Shearsman / Ottawa: BuschekBooks, 2011), translated by Erín Moure from the Galician of *Hordas de escritura* (Vigo, Spain: Xerais, 2008). By permission of Chus Pato.

———. *"from* While I'm Writing" is from "While I'm Writing," in
Secession/Insecession (Toronto: BookThug 2014), translated by Erín
Moure from the Galician of *Secesión* (Vigo, Spain: Xerais, 2008). By
permission of Chus Pato and BookThug.

Pessoa, Fernando. "XI Some Woman Out There Has a Piano" in *Sheep's
Vigil by a Fervent Person* (Toronto: House of Anansi Press, 2001),
translated by Erín Moure from the Portuguese of Alberto Caeiro's
O Guardador de Rebanhos, in *Athena* 4 and 5 (Lisbon, 1925). By
permission of House of Anansi Press.

Villazón, Emma. "Wavering Before the Water," in *The Capilano Review* 3,
no. 27 (Fall 2015), translated by Erín Moure from the Spanish of *Lumbre
de ciervos* (La Paz: La Hoguera, 2013). By permission of the Estate of
Emma Villazón.

Collaborative Works

Avasilichioaei, Oana and Erín Moure. *"from* Airways" in *Expeditions of a
Chimæra* (Toronto: BookThug, 2009). By permission of BookThug and
Oana Avasilichioaei.

Poetry of Erín Moure

from *Domestic Fuel* (1983), *Furious* (1988), *Search Procedures* (1996), *A
Frame of The Book / The Frame of A Book* (1999), *O Cidadán* (2002),
Little Theatres (2005), *O Cadoiro* (2007), *O Resplandor* (2010), *The
Unmemntioable* (2012), and *Kapusta* (2015) appears by permission of
House of Anansi Press at www.houseofanansi.com.

from *Empire, York Street* (Toronto: House of Anansi Press, 1979), *Wanted
Alive* (Toronto: House of Anansi Press, 1983), *WSW (West South West)*
(Montréal: Véhicule Press, 1989), and *Sheepish Beauty, Civilian Love*
(Montréal: Véhicule Press, 1992) appears by permission of Erín Moure.

from *Pillage Laud* (2011) and *Insecession* (2014), appears by permission of
BookThug at www.bookthug.ca.

Bibliography

Works Cited

Acker, Kathy. *Great Expectations.* New York: Grove Press, 1983.

Agamben, Giorgio. *Ce qui reste d'Auschwitz.* Translated by Pierre Alferi. Paris: Rivages Poches, 2003.

Ajens, Andrés. *quase flanders, quase extremadura.* Translated by Erín Moure. Cambridge, UK: CCCP, 2001; Victoria, BC: La Mano Izquierda, 2008.

Avasilichioaei, Oana. *Limbinal.* Vancouver: Talonbooks, 2015.

Beckett, Samuel. *The Poems, Short Fiction, and Criticism of Samuel Beckett.* Vol. 4 of Grove Centenary Edition. Translated by by Samuel Beckett. Edited by Paul Auster. Introduced by J. M. Coatzee. New York: Grove Press, 2006.

Bergvall, Caroline. "Propelled to the Edges of a Language's Freedom, and to the Depths of Its Collective Traumas." Interviewer, Eva Heisler. *Asymptote* (1 Jan. 2016). http://www.asymptotejournal.com

Bhabha, Homi K. *The Location of Culture.* London: Routledge, 1994.

Braidotti, Rosi. *Nomadic Subjects: Embodiment and Sexual Difference in Contemporary Feminist Theory.* Cambridge, UK: Columbia University Press, 1994.

Brook, Peter. *The Empty Space.* New York: Scribner, 1968.

Brossard, Nicole. *The Blue Books.* Translated by Patricia Claxton and Larry Shouldice. Toronto: Coach House Books, 2003.

———. *Installations.* Translated by Robert Majzels and Erín Moure. Winnipeg: Muses' Company, 2000.

———. *Museum of Bone and Water.* Translated by Robert Majzels and Erín Moure. Toronto: House of Anansi Press, 2003.

———. *Notebook of Roses and Civilization.* Translated by Robert Majzels and Erín Moure. Toronto: Coach House Books, 2007.

———. *White Piano.* Translated by Robert Majzels and Erín Moure. Toronto: Coach House Books, 2013.

Bueno, Wilson. *Mar Paraguayo.* São Paulo, Brazil: Iluminuras, 1992.

Butler, Judith. *Bodies That Matter.* New York: Routledge, 1993.

———. *Excitable Speech: A Politics of the Performative.* New York: Routledge, 1997.

Butling, Pauline and Susan Rudy. *Writing in Our Time: Canada's Radical*

Poetries in English (1957–2003). Waterloo, ON: Wilfrid Laurier University Press, 2005.

Cixous, Hélène and Clarice Lispector. *Reading with Clarice Lispector.* Translated by Verena Andermatt Conley. Minneapolis: Minnesota University Press, 1990.

Celan, Paul. *Threadsuns.* Translated by Pierre Joris. Los Angeles: Green Integer, 2000.

——. *Paul Celan: Selections.* Edited and translated by Pierre Joris. Oakland: University of California Press, 2005.

Cole, Norma. *Spinoza in Her Youth.* Richmond, CA: OmniDawn, 2002.

de Castro, Rosalía. *New Leaves.* Translated by Erín Moure from Galician of *Follas Novas* (1880). Sofia / Santiago de Compostela: Small Stations / Xunta de Galicia, 2016.

——. *Galician Songs.* Translated by Erín Moure from Galician of *Cantares Gallegos* (1872). Sofia / Santiago de Compostela: Small Stations / Xunta de Galicia, 2013.

Deleuze, Gilles. *Spinoza: Practical Philosophy.* Translated by Robert Hurley. San Francisco: City Lights, 1988.

Derrida, Jacques. *Of Grammatology.* Translated by Gayatri Chakravorty. Spivak. Baltimore: Johns Hopkins University Press, 1976.

——. *De l'hospitalité.* Paris: Calmann-Lévy, 1997.

——. *Schibboleth, pour Paul Celan.* Paris: Galilée, 1986.

——. *Mal d'Archive.* Paris: Galilée, 1995.

——. *Sovereignties in Question: The Poetics of Paul Celan.* Edited by Thomas Dutoit and Outi Pasanen. Translated by Thomas Dutoit, Jerry Glenn, Outi Pasanen, Philippe Romanski, and Joshua Wilner. New York: Fordham University Press, 2005.

Dopp, Jamie. "'A field of potentialities': Reading Erin Mouré." *Essays on Canadian Writing* 67 (Spring 1999): 261–287.

Dupré, Louise. *Just Like Her.* Translated by Erín Moure. Hamilton, ON: Wolsak and Wynn, 2011.

Fitzgerald, Heather. "Finesse into Mess: Entropy as Metaphor in the Queer Poetics of Erin Mouré." MA thesis, University of Calgary, December 1997. National Library of Canada: 0-612-312286-0.

Foucault, Michel. *L'ordre du discours.* Paris: Éditions Gallimard, 1971.

——. *L'Archéologie du savoir.* Paris: Éditions Gallimard, 1969.

——. *O que é um autor.* Translated by António Fernando Cascais and Eduardo Cordeiro. Lisbon: Passagens, 1992.

————. *The History of Sexuality: An Introduction*, vol. 1. Translated by Robert Hurley. New York: Vintage Editions, 1990.

García Lorca, Federico. *Four Puppet Plays, Divan Poems and Other Poems, Prose Poems and Dramatic Pieces, Play without a Title*. Translated by Edward Honig. Riverdale-on-Hudson, NY: Sheep Meadow Press, 1990.

————. *Obras V. Teatro II (Teatro Imposible); Cine, Música*. Edited by Miguel García Posada. Torrejón de Ardoz, Spain: Ediciones Akal, 1992.

————. *Romancero Gitano*. Edited by Emilio de Miguel. Madrid: Espasa Caple, 1995.

————. *Selected Verse*. Edited by Christopher Maurer. Translated by Francisco Aragon, Catherine Brown, Cola Franzen, Will Kirkland, William Bryant Logan, Christopher Maurer, Jerome Rothenberg, Grey Simon, Alan S. Trueblood, John K. Walsh, and Steven F. White. New York: Farrar Straus Giroux, 1995.

Gómez, Lupe. *Pornography*. Translated by Rebeca Lema Martínez and Erín Moure. In *Iberoromanic Studies in Literature and Translatology—Studies in Contemporary Literature*, vol. 1. Berlin: Frank and Timme, 2013.

Grosz, Elizabeth. *Volatile Bodies: Toward a Corporeal Feminism*. Bloomington: Indiana University Press, 1994.

Grubisic, Katia. "An Autobiography of Translation: An Interview with Erín Moure." *Montreal Review of Books* (Summer 2014). http://www .mtlreviewofbooks.ca

Hayles, N. Katherine. "Hypertext Hamlet." *Humanities* (September 1995): 23–28.

Harris, Claire. *Fables from the Women's Quarters*. Fredericton, NB: Goose Lane, 1995.

Hejinian, Lyn. *The Language of Inquiry*. Berkeley: University of California Press, 2000.

————. *My Life and My Life in the Nineties*. Middletown, CT: Wesleyan University Press, 2013.

Howe, Susan. *A Bibliography of the King's Book, or Eikon Basilike*. Providence, RI: Paradigm Press, 1989.

————. *Frame Structures: Early Poems, 1974–1979*. New York: New Directions, 1996.

————. *Singularities*. Middletown, CT: Wesleyan University Press, 1990.

————. *My Emily Dickinson*. Berkeley, CA: North Atlantic Books, 1985.

Irigaray, Luce. *This Sex Which Is Not One*. Translated by Catherine Porter. Ithaca, NY: Cornell University Press, 1985.

———. *An Ethics of Sexual Difference*. Translated by Carolyn Burke and Gillian C. Gill. Ithaca, NY. Cornell University Press, 1993.

Joyce, Michael. *Othermindedness: The Emergence of Network Culture*. Ann Arbor: University of Michigan Press, 2000.

———. *Of Two Minds: Hypertext Pedagogy and Poetics*. Ann Arbor: University of Michigan Press, 1995.

Kim, Myung Mi. *Under Flag*. Berkeley: Kelsey St. Press, 1991.

Kinsman, Gary and Patrizia Gentile. *The Canadian War on Queers: National Security as Sexual Regulation*. Vancouver: University of British Columbia Press, 2010.

Kristeva, Julia. *Revolution in Poetic Language*. Translated by Margaret Waller. New York: Columbia University Press, 1984.

Landale, Zoë, ed. *Shop Talk: The Vancouver Industrial Writers' Union*. Vancouver: Pulp Press, 1985.

Lévinas, Emmanuel. *Liberté et commandement*. Paris: Fata Morgana, 1994.

———. *Collected Philosophical Papers*. Translated by Alphonso Lingis. Pittsburgh, PA: Duquesne University Press, 1998.

Lowther, Pat. *The Collected Works of Pat Lowther*. Edited by Christine Wiesenthal. Edmonton: NeWest Press. 2010.

Lyotard, Jean-François. *The Differend: Phrases in Dispute*. Translated by G. Van Den Abbeele. Minneapolis: Minnesota University Press, 1998.

———. *Libidinal Economy*. Translated by Iain Hamilton Grant. Bloomington: Indiana University Press, 1993.

———. *La Confession d'Augustin*. Paris: Galilée, 1998.

Marinetti, F. T. "The Founding and Manifesto of Futurism." Translated by R. W. Flint, 19–24, in *The Documents of 20th Century Art: Futurist Manifestos*. Edited by Umbro Apollonio. New York: Viking, 1973.

Marlatt, Daphne. *Frames of a Story*. Toronto: The Ryerson Press, 1968.

Moure, Erín. *A Frame of The Book / The Frame of A Book*. Los Angeles: Sun & Moon; Toronto: House of Anansi Press, 1999.

———. *Domestic Fuel*. Toronto: House of Anansi Press, 1985.

———. *Empire, York Street*. Toronto: House of Anansi Press, 1979.

———. *Furious*. Toronto: House of Anansi Press, 1988.

———. *Kapusta*. Toronto: House of Anansi Press, 2015.

———. *Little Theatres*. Toronto: House of Anansi Press, 2005.

———. *My Beloved Wager: Essays from a Writing Practice*. Edited by Smaro Kamboureli. Edmonton: NeWest Press, 2009.

——. *O Cadoiro.* Toronto: House of Anansi Press, 2007.

——. *O Cidadán.* Toronto: House of Anansi Press, 2002.

——. *O Resplandor.* Toronto: House of Anansi Press, 2010.

——. *Pillage Laud.* Toronto: BookThug, 2011, and Moveable Type, 1999.

——. *Search Procedures.* Toronto: House of Anansi Press, 1996.

——. *Sheepish Beauty, Civilian Love.* Montréal: Véhicule Press, 1992.

——. *The Green Word: Selected Poems 1973–1992.* Toronto: Oxford University Press, 1999.

——. *The Unmemntioable.* Toronto: House of Anansi Press, 2012.

——. *Wanted Alive.* Toronto: House of Anansi Press, 1983.

——. *WSW (West South West).* Montréal: Véhicule Press, 1989.

Moure, Erín. *Insecession.* In one book with Chus Pato's *Secession.* Toronto: BookThug, 2014.

Moure, Erín and Oana Avasilichioaei. *Expeditions of a Chimæra.* Toronto: BookThug, 2009.

Nancy, Jean-Luc. *The Sense of the World.* Translated by Jeffrey S. Librett. Minneapolis: Minnesota University Press, 1997.

——. *La création du monde ou la mondialisation.* Paris: Galilée, 2002.

Nogueira, María Xesús, Laura Lojo, Manuela Palacios, eds. *Creation, Publishing, and Criticism: The Advance of Women's Writing.* Translated by Erín Moure (Galician chapters). Galician and Irish Studies series, vol. 2. General Editor Kathleen March. New York: Peter Lang, 2010.

Olson, Charles. "Projective Verse." In *Collected Prose,* edited by Donald Allen and Benjamin Friedlander, 239–249. Berkeley and Los Angeles: University of California Press, 1997.

Pato, Chus. *Secession.* Translated by Erín Moure. In one volume with Erín Moure's *Insecession.* Toronto: BookThug, 2014.

——. *Charenton.* Translated by Erín Moure. Exeter, UK: Shearsman / Ottawa: BuschekBooks, 2007.

——. *Flesh of Leviathan.* Translated by Erín Moure. San Francisco: Omnidawn, 2016.

——. *Hordes of Writing.* Translated by Erín Moure. Exeter, UK: Shearsman / Ottawa: BuschekBooks, 2011.

——. *m-Talá.* Translated by Erín Moure. Exeter, UK: Shearsman / Ottawa: BuschekBooks, 2009.

Pessoa, Fernando. *The Book of Disquiet.* Translated by Richard Zenith. New York: Penguin Books, 2002.

——. (as Alberto Caeiro). *Sheep's Vigil by a Fervent Person.* Translated by Eirin Moure from *O Guardador de Rebanhos*. Toronto: House of Anansi Press, 2001.

———. *Alberto Caeiro: Poesía*. Edited by Fernando Cabral Martíns and Richard Zenith. Lisbon: Assírio e Alvim, 2001.

Rancière, Jacques. *Aisthesis*. Paris: Galilée, 2011.

Russolo, Luigi. *The Art of Noises*. Translated by Barclay Brown. New York: Pendragon Press, 1986.

Scott, Gail. *Spare Parts*. Toronto: Coach House Press, 1981.

———. *Spaces Like Stairs*. Toronto: The Women's Press, 1989.

Shklovsky, Victor. "Art as Technique" (1917) in *Russian Formalist Criticism, Four Essays*. Translated and edited by Lee T. Lemon and Marion Reis, 3–24. Lincoln: University of Nebraska Press, 1965.

Stein, Gertrude. *Tender Buttons: Objects, Food, Rooms*. Auckland: Floating Press, 2009.

Svendsen, Linda, ed. *Words We Call Home: Celebrating Creative Writing at UBC*. Vancouver: University of British Columbia Press, 1990.

Théoret, France. *Bloody Mary*. Montréal: Les Herbes Rouges, 1984.

Villazón, Emma. *Lumbre de Ciervos*. La Paz, Bolivia: La Hoguera, 2013.

Webb, Phyllis. "The Crannies of Matter: Texture in Robin Blaser's Later 'Image-Nations.'" *Nothing But Brush Strokes: Selected Prose of Phyllis Webb*. Edited by Smaro Kamboureli. Edmonton: NeWest Press, 1995.

Wittig, Monique. *The Lesbian Body*. Translated by David Le Vay. New York: Morrow, 1975.

Further Reading

Selected Articles and Chapters by Erín Moure

Moure, Erín and Karis Shearer. "The Public Reading." In *Public Poetics: Critical Issues in Canadian Poetry and Poetics*, edited by Bart Vautour, Erin Wunker, Travis V. Mason, and Christl Verduyn, 271–287. Waterloo, ON: Wilfrid Laurier University Press, 2015.

Moure, Erín and Forrest Gander. "In Conclusion, Ajens: An Introduction in Two Voices." Preface to Ajens, Andrés. *Poetry After the Invention of America: Don't Light the Flower*. Essays translated from Spanish by Michelle Gil-Montero. New York: Palgrave Macmillan, 2011.

Moure, Erín and Caroline Bergvall. "O Yes." In *Antiphonies: Essays on Women's Experimental Poetries In Canada*, 167–176. Willowdale, ON: The Gig, 2008.

Moure, Erín and Chris Daniels. "An Exchange on Translation." In
Antiphonies: Essays on Women's Experimental Poetries in Canada,
177–183. Willowdale, ON: The Gig, 2008.

Moure, Erín. "Translation's_Homeopathic_Gestures." *Jacket2* (September
29, 2012–January 27, 2013). http://www.jacket2.org

———. "D'ailleurs, la page." In *Autopoéticas*, edited by Arturo Casas, Isaac
Lourido, and Laura Mariño, 365–367. Santiago de Compostela, Spain:
GAAP, 2012..

———. "A Year Later, I Am in Lilac Now." In *The Heart Does Break:
Canadian Writers on Grief and Mourning*, edited by George Bowering
and Jean Baird, 243–262. Toronto: Random House, 2009.

———. "The Fishes: Url Lanham." In *Lost Classics*, edited by Michael
Ondaatje, Michael Redhill, Linda Spalding, and Esta Spalding, 188–189.
Toronto: Knopf, 2000.

———. "The Capitulations, on Lani Maestro." In *Multiplier : Points de vue
sur l'art actuel des femmes*, 58–63. Montréal: La Centrale and Éditions
du remue-ménage, 1998.

Selected Articles and Chapters about Erín Moure

De Vuyst, Katelijne. "Leven is lezen: de poëtica van Erín Moure" or "Life
is Reading: The Poetics of Erín Moure." *Tijdschrift Filter* (Utrecht,
Netherlands) 19.3 (Fall 2012): 50–52.

Dudley, Stephanie. "The Making of the Independent Short Film, Teatriños:
Homenaxe ao mineral do repolo (Little Theatres: Homage to the
Mineral of Cabbage)." *Canada and Beyond* 2, no. 1–2 (December 2012).
http://www.canada-and-beyond.com/

Fitzpatrick, Ryan and Susan Rudy. "'These marked spaces lie beneath /
the alphabet': Readers, Borders, and Citizens in Erín Moure's Recent
Work." *Canadian Literature*, Issue 210/211, 21st Century Poetics
(Autumn/Winter 2011): 60–74.

Hooper, Kirsty. "Towards a Poetics of Relation? Ramiro Fonte, Xavier
Queipo, Erín Moure." In *Writing Galicia into the World: New
Cartographies, New Poetics*, 139–170. Liverpool, UK: Liverpool
University Press, 2011.

Jacques, Melissa. "The Indignity of Speaking: the Poetics of Representation
in Erin Mouré's 'Seebe.'" *Canadian Poetry* 47 (Fall/Winter 2000).

Kunin, Aaron. "Moure's Abrasions." In *Eleven More American Women
Poets in the 21st Century: Poetics across North America*, edited by

Claudia Rankine and Lisa Sewell, 171–188. Middletown, CT: Wesleyan University Press, 2012.

MacDonald, Tanis. "Elegy of Refusal: Erin Mouré's *Furious.*" In *The Daughter's Way: Canadian Women's Paternal Elegies*, 209–234. Waterloo, ON: Wilfrid Laurier University Press, 2012.

Maguire, Shannon. "Parasite Poetics: Noise and Queer Hospitality in Erín Moure's *O Cidadán.*" *Canadian Literature* 224 (Spring 2015). Issue on "Queer Frontiers."

Markotić, Nicole. "False Friends / Global Friends," In *Global Neo-Imperialism and National Resistance*, edited by Belén Martín Lucas and Ana Bringas López, 217–222. Vigo, Spain: University of Vigo Press, 2004.

McCance, Dawne. "Crossings: Interview with Erín Moure." *Mosaic* 36.4 (2003): 1–16.

Moyes, Lianne. "Acts of Citizenship: Erin Mouré's *O Cidadán* and the Limits Of Worldliness." In *Trans.Can.Lit: Resituating the Study of Canadian Literature*, edited by Smaro Kamboureli and Roy Miki, 111–128. Waterloo, ON: Wilfrid Laurier University Press, 2007.

———. "Local-Global! : Montréal dans la poésie de Robyn Sarah, Mary di Michele et Erin Mouré," *Voix et Images*, 30, no. 3 (Spring 2005): 113–132.

Nichols, Miriam. "Toward a Poetics of the Commons: *O Cidadán* and *Occasional Work.*" In *Antiphonies: Essays on Women's Experimental Poetries*, 146–166. Willowdale, ON: The Gig, 2008.

Quartermain, Meredith. "T'ang's Bathtub: Innovative Work by Four Canadian Poets." *Canadian Literature*, Issue 210/211, 21st Century Poetics (Autumn/Winter 2011): 116–132.

Rudy, Susan. "Por que pós-modernismo agora? Com vistas à poesia de enactment." Translated by Maria Lúcia Milléo Martins. *Ilha do Desterro* (Florianópolis, Brazil) 56 (JanJune 2009): 73–91.

———. "what can atmosphere with / vocabularies delight? Excessively Reading Erin Mouré." In *Writing in Our Time: Canada's Radical Poetries in English (1957–2003)*. Edited by Pauline Butling and Susan Rudy, 205–216. Waterloo, ON: Wilfred Laurier University Press, 2005.

Skibsrud, Johanna. "If We Dare To": Border Crossings in Erin Mouré's *O Cidadán.*" *The Brock Review* 11, no. 1 (2010): 15–27.

Skoulding, Zoë. "Erín Moure's Irruptive Citizenship." Chap. 6 in *Contemporary Women's Poetry & Urban Space: Experimental Cities*. New York-London: Palgrave Macmillan, 2013.

Spinosa, Danielle. "Sleeping in the Library: Susan Howe and Erin Mouré." *[Generic Pronoun] Creates: Anarchism, Authorship, Experiment.* 245–322. Dissertation, York University, 2015. http://yorkspace.library.yorku.ca/xmlui/handle/10315/30034

Williams, Dominic and Milena Marinkova. "Affective Trans-scapes: Affect, Translation, and Landscape in Erín Moure's *The Unmemntioable*." *Contemporary Women's Writing* 9, no. 1 (2015): 73–92. http://www.cww.oxfordjournals.org

Zolf, Rachel. "'Like plugging into an electric circuit': Fingering Out Erín Moure's Lesbo-Digit-O! Smut Poems." *Canadian Literature*, 210/211, 21st Century Poetics (Autumn/Winter 2011): 230–240.

ERÍN MOURE is a Canadian poet and translator of poetry. Three-time finalist for the Griffin Prize, and winner of the Governor General's Award for poetry, her eighteen books include the poetry of *Furious, O Cidadán, Little Theatres, O Resplandor, The Unmemntioable,* and *Kapusta,* and the essays of *My Beloved Wager.* She has translated or cotranslated sixteen books of poetry, and holds two honorary doctorates, from Brandon University (Canada) and the University of Vigo (Spain). She first crossed the Canada–US border from Alberta in 1964 to eat a July 4th hot dog at a community picnic in Great Falls, Montana, and has been border-crossing ever since. Moure lives in Montreal.

SHANNON MAGUIRE is an assistant professor in the Department of English at the University of Calgary. The author of two collections of poetry, *fur(l) parachute* and *Myrmurs: An Exploded Sestina,* she has been a finalist for the Robert Kroetsch Award for Innovative Poetry and the bpNichol Chapbook Award.